Joy Even on Your Worst Days

Joy Even on Your Worst Days

Wisdom from Philippians

Tom Are Jr.

RESOURCE *Publications* · Eugene, Oregon

JOY EVEN ON YOUR WORST DAYS
Wisdom from Philippians

Resource Publications
An Imprint of Wipf and Stock Publishers
199 W. 8th Ave., Suite 3
Eugene, OR 97401

www.wipfandstock.com

PAPERBACK ISBN: 978-1-6667-1126-4
HARDCOVER ISBN: 978-1-6667-1127-1
EBOOK ISBN: 978-1-6667-1128-8

09/03/21

For Carol:
when it comes to joy,
she is my best teacher.

Contents

Contents

Conversations With God: Joy

God," I asked, "What brings you joy?"

"Oh, my child," God said. "The list is so long.
> Hearing you say my name and seeing you soak in this beautiful creation bring me joy.
> When you stand with family, neighbors, and strangers, and sing or work together, my heart risks overflowing with joy.
> When you remember the children, and the quiet, and the hurting—I swear my heart could take flight."

"And when your heart takes flight, " I asked, leaning forward with curiosity, "then what happens?"

And God leaned back and laughed the most musical, heart-filled, soul-reaching laugh I'd ever heard, and that's when I remembered—joy is contagious, and it is a gift. And then I started singing.

—Sarah Are

To include this poem makes the writer of this book not only a grateful but also a very proud father.

Joy Even on Your Worst Days video series and study guide for small group discussion is available from Village Presbyterian Church at Villagepres.org.

Acknowledgments

I HAVE ALWAYS KNOWN that a preacher never steps into the pulpit alone. There is always a cloud of witnesses who stands there with him or her. In this first effort, I have learned the same is true for those who write a book. Often acknowledgments mention those who helped with the writing and shaping of the book. In this case, that means those who helped with the shaping of the writer.

I am grateful for the communities that formed me in faith and taught me how to be a pastor. That includes three small congregations in western Virginia—Falling Spring, Sinking Spring, and Greenwood—for they took me in as a seminary intern and convinced me that I was not called to teach but to spend my days sharing this faith with congregations. I am grateful for the saints of the Westminster Presbyterian Church in Charleston, South Carolina, the first congregation I served. They took me in when I was green as a spring lawn. For the congregations of Seven Oaks Presbyterian Church in Columbia, South Carolina, and Riverside Presbyterian Church in Jacksonville, Florida, I am grateful for the courage they showed in ministry and the room they gave me to find my voice. And finally, the Village Presbyterian Church in Prairie Village, Kansas. I have learned more about the church and about ministry in the seventeen years we have spent together than in the rest of my life. These are the congregations that taught me what it is to be a pastor or, as they say in my family, a preacher.

I am thankful to my assistant Marsha Hansen, who read this manuscript, who knows how little I love details, and who takes care of so many of them for me. I thank my friend Rev. Dr. Scott Black Johnston and my friend and colleague Rev. Dr. Rodger Nishioka, both of whom read portions of this manuscript and offered encouragement along the way. I am grateful to my friends in *The Moveable Feast*, a preaching study group, who have taught me not simply how to preach but, more importantly, that preaching matters. I thank Rev. Bob Dunham, my first colleague and boss. He and I are as different as silk and burlap, and he is silk. The wisdom he shared with me in my early days of ministry has only increased in value through the years.

I am grateful for Sarah and Nathan, my children, for the ways you remind me daily of the goodness of God. For Carol, who listens to me preach every Sunday and who lives this faith with more integrity than I ever do. Lastly, I am grateful for my father, Rev. Tom Are Sr., who died during this writing. He was a giant in my life and the lives of many others. I am grateful that the good work that God began in him has been brought to completion.

Introduction

Why Paul?

PAUL HAS TAUGHT ME much, and I am grateful for his words, although I don't know if I would want to meet him for lunch. He can be rather hard to take at times. He's arrogant and, in some ways, sees the world so differently than I do, I wonder what we might say to one another, were we to find ourselves at lunch together. Part of that is Paul, part of that is me, but it is mostly the two thousand years that lie between us. After all, for at least a portion of his life, and probably the portion during which he wrote this letter, Paul lived in the same zip code with Caesar; for me, Caesar is just a salad. The passing of a couple millennia means Paul could not imagine a world that I take for granted. Paul was a man of his times. We all are defined and in ways confined by our times. In some ways, Paul was ahead of his time. But he was not so far ahead of his time that he could imagine the world we inhabit. Paul had no way to conceive of Adam Smith's capitalism or Galileo's heliocentrism or the modern capacity to curate a self online, all of which constitute the nitrogen and oxygen of the cultural atmosphere in which we live. As much as any of that, it would push Paul beyond his imaginative capacities to conceive of what David Brooks calls a hyper-individualism that is the hub of contemporary Western culture.[1] So we can't expect to be on the same page with the apostle in every circumstance. Nevertheless, there were folks in the early church who not only fell in love with this letter but were convinced that we would, too. So they kept it and handed it down, generation by generation. At the end of the day, particularly a hard day, I am grateful they did.

My appreciation for Paul has come slowly. I am a preacher who is drawn more to the stories of Scripture than to the letters. To complicate

1. Brooks, *Second Mountain*, xvii.

1

matters, all these letters were written to someone else. And yet, over time, the apostle has gifted me with some aspects of my faith that I hadn't even recognized I needed. His letter to the Philippians has become a holy word for me. Those old saints from the early church, who kept this letter alive and passed it down to us—it turns out they were right about the power of this short correspondence. This is a letter I have fallen in love with.

In reading this letter, it helps to remember that Paul first had to push these words through the bars of his prison cell. The fact that this is prison mail provides a basis for the admiration that you will find in these pages. Not every verse is about being incarcerated, but it is clear that the apostle would prefer to visit with his friends in Philippi than to waste away in jail. Given that such a visit was an impossibility, and Zoom was yet to be invented, a letter would have to suffice. While there are only a few hints of struggle in the epistle, it was not an easy time for the apostle. He celebrates that "what has happened to me has actually helped to spread the gospel." But it still happened to him, and what happened was prison. I don't know if this was Paul's worst day, but it couldn't have been his best day.

After serving congregations for over thirty years, I, like everyone who might read this, have my own stories of those who have been pushed up against the brutal edges of life. As a pastor, I have learned, if you give life enough time, you will find yourself by a hospital bed praying against some killer disease. You will find yourself singing "For All the Saints" at a service for a child who didn't live long enough to learn to sing "Jesus Loves Me." You will have coffee with a man who has lost his job or visit with a child whose mother has died. You will pray with a friend whose brother was shot or whose son just didn't wake up one morning or who is fighting a losing battle with alcohol. You will sit through a repetitive visit with someone whose memories have been forwarded ahead to glory, leaving a diminished and more simple self waiting to catch up. Everyone has stories like these, because the cruel hammer of suffering falls on every life at one time or another.

Sometimes the biggest source of suffering comes not from the twists and turns of external circumstances but in the consequences that result from our own choices. There is evidence in the epistle that there was disagreement in the Philippian congregation. It doesn't appear to be as significant as in Corinth, for example, but it was significant enough for Paul to address it. The truth is, in every letter Paul writes, from Romans to Philemon, Paul speaks of, even pleads for, the unity of the church. He consistently labors to keep the church family together. This tells us at least two things.

The first is that there is something basically Christian about unity. To borrow from the Gospel of John, the world will know we are followers of Jesus by our love for one another. When the world looks at the church and sees not love for one another but conflict, it is hard for them to see Jesus alive in the church.

The second thing Paul's repeated exhortation to unity reveals is that love for one another has been challenging for a long time. This ancient reality is essentially contemporary. Unity never comes easily. It is not just the church's struggle to make up our minds on inclusion of the LGBTQ community or how to respond to the realities of climate change or the immigrants in our midst or the persistent battles with racism in American culture. Most congregations recognize matters like these are of great importance and that faith requires that we engage them with "energy, intelligence, imagination and love."[2] And yet congregations tread with care because the risk of division always awaits. Sadly, the church often fractures over things not nearly as weighty as these. We are good at disagreeing on the time for worship or whether communion includes juice or wine or what kind of coffee to serve after service. If you have been in a congregation where these disagreements become definitive of the community, perhaps even leading to schism, then you know it's the worst kind of pain for the church. It is also the poorest witness to the gospel we could offer to the community outside the church.

When life becomes complicated by the realities of suffering, whether the pain comes from unavoidable circumstances or from consequences we bring on ourselves, it is a faithful response to simply sit with folks while their hearts are tender. We don't have to talk right away, and sometimes it's best just to sit in silence. The ministry of presence is a healing power. With almost twenty-five chapters of apparently unending advice from Job's friends, I imagine Job would have loved to have his friends just shut up for a chapter or two. To simply sit with folks when their world has fallen apart is an important expression of love. But in time, the pain of life raises questions that cannot and should not be ignored. As Tom Long has said, "Just because [we] do not have a silver bullet, an 'Aha!' answer to the problem of suffering that will make it all plain, does not mean that we do not have a long history of ways of thinking this issue through."[3] When life falls apart, talking about it helps. Talking about it theologically helps even more.

---

2. This phrase is a portion of an ordination vow in the Presbyterian Church (USA).

3. Long, *What Shall We Say*, 30.

You, no doubt, have a story of pain. Everyone does. Paul did, too. Paul was well acquainted with the rougher edges of life. We learn more about this from Acts than we do from his letters, but it appears his life was relatively smooth, until the risen Christ bumped into him on the Damascus road. After that, few days were free from complication. His seemingly unwavering devotion to Jesus Christ and his confidence that God had called him to speak grace to gentiles (folks like me) emboldened him in the face of many hardships, including frequent imprisonments. It is from the dank cell of one of his imprisonments that Paul wrote this letter.

Philippians is jail mail. As such, we might expect the letter to carry a tone of regret or disappointment or even resentment, but the consistent vibe of this letter is joy. I find that both remarkable and important. Paul's joy is a joy that rises up even when the circumstances of life are disappointing. It is this joy, or a hunger for it, that has led me to write this little book. I write not because I am like Paul, either in the pervasiveness of his suffering nor in the depth of his joy; I write because, in this aspect, I would like to be more like him. I want to know joy even when it is difficult, even on the worst days.

The culture in which we live is not a particularly joyful culture. We are better at anger and understandably so. There is a lot of fear, and that's not likely to change. The macro story of the Western world is that we are to invest ourselves in pursuing a good life, which is defined by a collection of positive circumstances: small responsibilities, big bank accounts, good health, lots of friends who are always easy to get along with, and an economic status that allows us to be comfortable. This narrative is incredibly powerful and has led us to an assumption about life: that suffering is an aberration to normal life. We assume suffering is an intrusion into the way life is supposed to be. Therefore, when suffering comes—and it always comes—it is something we must explain as we somehow fit the broken pieces of our lives together in a logical fashion. But what if the assumption that a normal life is one free from suffering is wrong?

A Bit of My Story

My own life has largely been a life of privilege. I was born into a family who loved me and took me to church. My parents made sure I was afforded an education. I have always had a job. I fell in love and married up, as my side of the family says. I'm a white guy in a world that puts us at the front of the line. And the only times I have been to jail were to visit. I am mindful that these privileges mean that most people in this world face challenges that I can only try to understand. Some who have faced such challenges, whom I have come to know either in the flesh or through study, have become my teachers in the way that they have demonstrated joy in the face of hardship. Some of these teachers I have included in the following chapters. On the whole, therefore, it is less from an experience of deep personal suffering but, rather, a recognition that faith requires attentiveness to the suffering of others that informs these pages. Nevertheless, no life is completely devoid of heartbreak.

Gene is my big little brother. That's how he describes himself. That means he is the second of four children and the middle of three brothers. So he's little to me and big to his baby brother, Jim. Gene is a special needs kid who has become a special needs adult. He never forgets my birthday, and he loves to talk on the phone. Gene's mind is simple. He will never read a book, not even a children's book. Still, it's easy to catch him with a book open as he copies letters from the book into a spiral notebook. He has no idea what the words say, but he likes the copying. He says he is doing his homework. He is also a seriously funny man. With every conversation, he says something that causes me to laugh out loud. Whenever I gather with my other siblings, we all rehearse our Gene stories. Gene is the source of profound joy in my life. But that joy is complicated. There is not a thing I have written here that he could comprehend, and for the longest time I was more than a little angry at God, that God would allow or cause or accept such limitations placed on my big little brother. Over the years (decades really), I have lost my anger. More importantly, I have lost my desire for an explanation of this and of most innocent suffering in the world. There have been times I have yearned for an answer or explanation, but no longer. Truth be told, were someone to provide an answer or a reason why my big little brother was born the way he was, I think I would find it irrelevant at best and insulting at worst. Suffering is not something we explain. To do so implies that if we look hard enough, we will find the reason the innocent should suffer. If there is a reason the innocent should suffer, well then, it must be a good thing. To declare that someone's suffering happens for this reason or that reason suggests that, at the end of the day, what we experience is not really suffering but a good thing, or at least an acceptable thing.

I resonate with Dr. Kate Bowler, associate professor of church history at Duke Divinity School. In the midst of her scholarly work on the prosperity gospel—a theology that promises that through faith, everything will work out just fine—she got cancer. Dr. Bowler was thirty-five years of age. She chronicled her journey and her courageous battle with cancer, including the support and responses from those around her. She writes: "Most everyone I meet is dying to make me certain. They want me to know, without a doubt, that there is a hidden logic to this seeming chaos. Even when I was still in the hospital, a neighbor came to the door and told my husband that everything happens for a reason.

"'I'd love to hear it,' he replied.

"'Pardon?' she said, startled.

"'The reason my wife is dying,' he said."[4]

Her neighbor couldn't provide a reason, and the truth is, a reason is the last thing he wanted. Suffering is not something we explain so much as something we battle.

A Reliable Witness

I think Christian faith is short on explanations for suffering. But I think Christian faith is strong on responses to suffering. Our faith calls us to battle suffering in this world. I think Paul teaches us a little of what life is like in the battle.

Philippians is not the book of Job. Philippians does not address innocent suffering head-on. And yet, woven through this letter, we encounter the suffering of Paul, his co-workers, and the Philippian congregation, while central to the letter is the suffering of Christ. Paul seems absolutely unsurprised not only that he is oppressed but also that his faith is the reason he suffers. If he asks a question, it is not why, but, rather, what now. He answers this unspoken question with a song of joy that rises up from the prison cell. He is instructive to us when we find ourselves locked in the prisons of contemporary life, captured by the harsh circumstances of the day, chained to situations that erode human flourishing, or confined by the consequences of the long march of sin through every generation. When life falls apart, Tom Long says, we yearn for a reliable witness.[5] A reliable witness is someone with the wisdom and experience to talk with us about the way forward.

4. Bowler, *Everything Happens*, 112.
5. Long, *What Shall We Say*, 32.

To say it again, when it comes to suffering, Christian faith is short on answers as to why but consistently calls us to battle suffering. If I understand this letter, Paul battles. This book is called *Joy Even on Your Worst Days*. But let me be clear, there is no silver bullet here. There is no easy fix or four-step system to make it all better. There is just the testimony of an ordinary man with a trust in God, who writes from prison to all who are in Christ, to offer us a witness. I find it a reliable witness. When suffering comes to you (and if it hasn't yet, it will), Paul would say, your suffering is not evidence that God has stepped away, or is taking a nap, or has forgotten who you are. No, suffering is the battlefield. Suffering is not actually an aberration. Where did we ever get that idea, given that the one we worship was crucified? Suffering is the circumstance that persons of faith engage, and even if we cannot change the circumstance, we nevertheless endeavor to sing a song of joy through the dark of night. It is a song that bears witness to our trust that the morning is coming.

The Dalai Lama and Archbishop Desmond Tutu teamed up to write a book about joy. The Dalai Lama is the title given to the most prominent spiritual guide in the yellow hat school of Tibetan Buddhism. He is a refugee in India, as he is unwelcomed in Tibet. Archbishop Tutu is a winner of a Nobel Peace Prize and was a champion in the fight against apartheid. He was the visionary behind the Truth and Reconciliation Commission in post-apartheid South Africa. Needless to say, both these men have faced the darkest nights and carried unbearable burdens of human suffering. And yet, when in their presence, it is hard to miss the spirit of joy that exudes from them both. Tutu reflected on joy this way: "Discovering more joy does not, I'm sorry to say, . . . save us from the inevitability of hardship and heartbreak. In fact, we may cry more easily, but we will laugh more easily, too. Perhaps we are just more alive. Yet as we discover more joy, we can face suffering in a way that ennobles rather than embitters. We have hardship without becoming hard. We have heartbreak without being broken."[6]

Paul writes this letter of joy from prison. Paul provides no step-by-step process to find joy when your heart is broken, but he does offer a testimony to the power of the grace of God that makes it possible, even when life has disappointed us, to find joy on your worst days.

This writing is not a commentary. There has been no deep dive into the Greek language nor a thorough survey of commentary offerings, although a smattering of both will appear. While specific verses will be discussed,

6. Lama et al., *Book of Joy*, 12.

there is no attempt to cover every verse, like a traditional commentary. This is a reflection on the text, offered by a preacher who cares about the text and the way it can shape faith in our own time. It is hoped that what is offered here will be a source of encouragement for folks who carry with them to Sunday morning worship honest questions as they seek to integrate the circumstances of their lives with the good news they hear proclaimed in worship. It is also hoped that those who do the proclaiming might find a helpful word here as well. I hold a profound appreciation for those who spend Tuesday mornings, Thursday afternoons, and more than a few Saturday nights in search for the words that will proclaim hope and love on a given Sunday morning. For most preachers, finding the words that can honestly name the reality of the world in which we live and also cultivate the holy imagination for the world that God intends—finding these faithful words is a blessed wonder and an undeniable burden. If the thoughts and observations of this preacher provide any encouragement in this sacred and ordinary task, it would be a joy. These pages are offered not because this preacher has insight that is unique, but because there is value in remembering and reciting the old, old story. Hans Küng wrote an extensive theology, and in the preface, he stated, "This book was written, not because the author thinks he is a good Christian, but because he thinks that being a Christian is a particularly good thing."[7] These few pages are offered in that same spirit. I am not much like the apostle we meet in Philippians, but I would like to be. By the grace of God, whether today is a good day or not, maybe it can be a day of joy.

7. Küng, *On Being a Christian*, 20.

CHAPTER 1

The Promised Day of Christ

PAUL LOVES THE CONGREGATION in Philippi. They aren't a perfect bunch, but Paul is proud of them, and it shows. Paul is a source of strength for them, but they too are an encouragement for Paul.

As Paul writes this letter, he is in trouble. He is jailed under a capital charge. We might expect that a letter that has been pushed through the prison bars would carry a tone of anxiety or regret, but Philippians is a letter that sings like a song of joy.

We all have joyous days; we all have painful days as well. But this letter from Paul offers testimony that it is possible to know joy even on your worst days. It may take a while. To speak of joy on your worst days is not a statement of timing—that is, joy seldom shows up at the same moment heartbreak occurs. To speak of joy on your worst days is to acknowledge that if joy is real, it must be powerful enough to address your worst days. That will likely take some time. Maybe Paul wrote a few rough drafts of the Philippian letter, lost to us now, that were filled with lament, rage, and disappointment. Maybe. But sooner or later, by the grace of God, Paul learns to rest in a joy that he knows even in prison.

Pisteuo!

Mr. Dunning spun the basketball on his finger, and drops of water flew off the surface, flying in every direction. Mr. Dunning was the sixth-grade science teacher at Hawthorne Elementary School. He was also the physical education teacher, and basketball was his favorite sport. This struck us as an odd choice, as most of the sixth graders were taller than Mr. Dunning. He barked orders like he had been a drill sergeant before he chose to spend his days teaching science to eleven-year-old kids. As he spun the ball, he talked about gravity. He told us the earth spins just like the basketball on his finger, and that we are like the drops of water on the surface of the ball. As the earth spins around, the reason we don't fly off in the general direction of Venus is because gravity holds us in place. Even though the object lesson is one I still remember, I have never fully understood gravity. I know about Sir Isaac Newton under the apple tree, but my knowledge of just how this law of physics works is quite limited. Yet, even with my pitiful understanding of this force, I still trust it.

One summer, my wife and I packed our kids in our minivan and headed west to take in some sights I had never seen. We hiked in Rocky Mountain National Park and then headed south to Pikes Peak. Pikes Peak is one of over fifty mountains in Colorado that rises over fourteen thousand feet above sea level. Some people climb these mountains simply because they are fourteeners, but not us. We took the cog train to the top. We were there on the Fourth of July and it was snowing at the top. (I don't want to live anyplace where it snows on July Fourth.) We traveled further southwest and there climbed among the cliff dwellings at Mesa Verde, where Pueblo Native Americans once lived. We then headed to our ultimate destination: the Grand Canyon. I was not prepared. The beauty is nothing less than breathtaking. For millions of years, the Colorado River and her tributaries have been excavating soil and rock, leaving an unparalleled sculpted canyon. No jigsaw puzzle depiction or National Geographic photo can prepare you for the stunning beauty of the canyon. Its colors and contrasts are striking. In some places, it is eighteen miles across and over a mile deep. But what surprised me even more than the beauty is the fact that there are no guard rails. Even though the edge can drop straight down hundreds of feet, there are no safety rails. You can walk right up to the edge and dangle your toes over the cliff, if you are the type. It turns out, I am not the type. Why? I have a high confidence in gravity. It's not the heights that frighten me, it's the idea of falling. Even though I don't fully understand how gravity works, I trust it. Because I trust it, gravity shapes my choices.

Faith is like gravity. It influences our choices; at least, it should. For the longest time, I considered faith to be primarily an intellectual exercise. I understood faithfulness as the pursuit of right doctrine. I had a seminary professor who taught us that a good theologian would master the data of theology. I failed to see that even more important than doctrine were the choices made each day. When the scribe asked Jesus, "Which is the first commandment?" Jesus didn't respond with a doctrinal statement. Jesus said, love God with all that you are, and love your neighbor as yourself. More than getting our doctrine right, following Christ—or as Paul likes to say, being in Christ—is about getting our relationships right. I am still an advocate of the stewardship of the mind. Doctrine matters, but its purpose is to shape how we engage our relationships. What we think or believe should show up in our choices. In the Greek language, the word *pisteuo* is translated "I believe." But *pisteuo* is to believe in the sense of being convinced of or to trust. Trust is a little different than belief. Belief is an intellectual category. Often when we speak of believing something, we are speaking of what we think. But if we trust something, it shapes our choices. I can believe forgiveness is a good thing, but if I trust it, I might actually forgive someone.

Paul writes to a small collection of Christians we know as the Philippians. They are, for those of us who profess faith in Christ, our ancestors. The Philippians had some troubles of their own. They had opponents (Phil 1:28), and surprising to no one who has ever been in a church—or any other group, for that matter—they had disagreements among themselves (Phil 4:2). Both of these realities caused trouble in the church. Trouble was something the apostle knew about. He writes to persuade and inspire them on any day, but particularly on hard days, to trust the lordship of Jesus Christ.

Philippians 1:1–2

Paul and Timothy, servants of Christ Jesus,
    To all the saints in Christ Jesus who are in Philippi, with the bishops and deacons:
    2Grace to you and peace from God our Father and the Lord Jesus Christ.

Identity Matters

There are a variety of ways I could introduce myself to someone I was meeting for the first time. I am a pastor, and I am a big baseball fan, as long as there is no cheating involved in the game. Other than the addition of junior, I have the same name as my dad. I'm a father and very proud of my two young adult children. I am a husband and have been blessed to be married to a remarkable woman for over thirty years. Depending on the context, I can offer a variety of descriptors. But after we know one another, I prefer to simply be called Tom.

In Paul's day, letter writing began by identifying the writer. This letter is from Paul and Timothy. This does not suggest that Timothy is a co-author, but does indicate that not even apostles go it alone.

It should not be glossed over that Paul adds, "servants of Christ Jesus." It would be enough to identify himself simply as Paul. The Philippians know him and love him. They need no further descriptor—unless, of course, for some reason, they do. To remind the Philippians that Paul and Timothy are servants of Christ is not new information; it is reaffirmation. Paul cannot speak of himself, and we will see that he cannot speak of the Christians in Philippi, without speaking of their relationship to Jesus Christ. Often Paul identifies himself as an apostle (1 Cor. 1:1; 1 Cor. 1:1; Gal 1:1). Sometimes he sees himself as a prisoner of Christ Jesus (Phlm 1). But here Paul claims to be a servant of Christ Jesus.

Servant sounds demeaning to our modern ear. No one wants to be a servant; we want to be free. Paul would agree, but he has a different understanding of freedom. In contemporary America, there is a widely held conviction that freedom is the capacity to do what I want, when I want, as I want. Like the prodigal who yearns to shake off the constraints of the old homeplace and discover real life, we set out to live an authentic life, a life of our own choosing. James K. A. Smith describes it this way: "It doesn't matter what you choose; what matters is that you choose. Freedom is getting to make up what counts as the Good for yourself."[1] Is there anything more important than my capacity to choose the way I walk life's road? Paul would say, yes! Paul will speak with passion about the importance of the choices we make, but those choices are first shaped by the fact that we belong to Christ. When choice is the altar before which life bows down, it is always a solo act. It is always my choice. Paul is convinced that life is not fully human when we are alone. The human life that flourishes is the person who knows we are not alone; we belong. When Paul identifies himself as a servant, he is asserting that "Christ has made me his own" (Phil 3:12). To be a servant of Christ is the most meaningful way to live a life. A servant is a humble person, and as we will see, when we live in humility, we bear a Christlike posture. Paul will say that Christ himself came into the world as a servant (Phil

1. Smith, *On the Road*, 62.

2:7). There is nothing demeaning in walking through this world as an echo of Christ. Being Christ's servant brings Paul joy. Most of all, Paul is claiming an identity that stands in strong contrast to how others around him know him or think they know him. Others would identify Paul as a prisoner of Caesar, but Paul rejects that designation as an ultimate descriptor. It is not what Caesar can do to him but what Christ has done for him that makes Paul who he is. Caesar simply lacks the power to change the truth that Paul is a servant of Christ Jesus. Daniel Migliore says, Paul "knows himself and his purpose in life as fully and irrevocably defined by his relationship to Christ."[2] Paul writes to remind the church—and perhaps to remind himself as well—that he belongs to Christ. When you are in Caesar's prison, it is no small thing to remember who you really are.

Once we know who is writing a letter, the second item in a letter written in Paul's day was an identification of the reader. The Philippian congregation was founded by Paul. Philippi bears its name from Philip II of Macedon, who conquered the region and built a city to name after himself. The Greek cultural roots trace to this fourth-century BCE conquest. By the time Paul came to Philippi, it was a Roman colony, and many from the Italian peninsula had come to settle the region. They introduced worship of the Roman emperor.

When Paul identifies the congregation, he does not point to their mixture of Greek and Roman backgrounds, but, rather, he identifies them as saints. I don't know what that word makes you think of, but I don't know many folks who describe themselves as saints. But Paul would encourage you to think of yourself in just that way. For us, the term saint identifies those who have excelled in living Christian faith. The saints in this world include Mother Teresa and Oscar Romero. Martin Luther King Jr, Dietrich Bonhoeffer, Desmond Tutu, and Dorothy Day are saints in my book. But saints are not limited to those whom the world knows. You could make a list of folks in your life who have inspired you, taught you, and encouraged you in a life of faith. They, too, are saints. The saints in your life may include a grandparent or a teacher, perhaps a mentor or just a person in your life who has shown you what grace looks like. To the rest of the world, the folks on your list may be unknown, but because they have been instruments of grace in your life, they are saints.

We don't often find our way to faith on our own. For most of us, there is a cloud of witnesses (Heb 12:1) who have loved us into the faith. We all

---

2. Migliore, *Philippians and Philemon*, 21.

need those people, and even if the world would not recognize them as such, we know them as the saints in our lives.

When Paul uses the word saint, he is not talking about the spiritually elite. He is not talking about those who have excelled in a life of faith. When Paul uses the word saint, he is talking about all of us. For Paul, a saint is someone who has been claimed by grace and also lives as an instrument of God's grace. Therefore, to call someone a saint, as Paul understands it, says less about their faithfulness and more about God's grace. The Philippian saints are graced ones. Paul reminds them that their truest identity is that they are saints. It's true of us as well. Paul is reminding us who we are. We are those defined by the grace of God: saints.

It was the first time I had ever held car keys. I was not allowed to put them to use. I didn't even know what they were. I was not yet a year old. My father gave me his keys in a desperate effort to distract me. I was bored, or maybe uncomfortable, or perhaps just impatient, but for some reason, I was quite wiggly at an inconvenient time to be wiggly. My parents had carried me to a small Gothic-style sanctuary and presented me for the sacrament of baptism. They held me in front of an attentive congregation, who probably thought I was cute in the way all babies mildly misbehaving are cute. A pastor by the name of Eade placed water on my head and said out loud to the saints gathered on that Sunday morning that I was not merely the firstborn son of Tom and Peggy, but I was actually a child of God. Apparently, I was uninterested. I can be forgiven for that, as I was too young to know the first thing about God. I didn't even know what car keys were for. I wouldn't remember this moment, nor any of the people in that congregation, as we moved to another community about the time I learned to walk. But I didn't belong to God because of anything I knew. It was announced that I belonged to God not because of any goodness or love in my heart but because of the love in God's heart. The love in God's heart is a love that calls us all by name and will never let us go. While I don't remember that sultry Sunday in Mississippi, I have been told the story, and I am forever grateful, because it reminds me who I really am.

I'm still the firstborn son of Tom and Peggy, and I am grateful for that. I am a pastor and a baseball fan. I am an obnoxiously proud dad. I like to dabble in woodworking, and there was a season in my life when I could play "Leader of the Band" or "Blackbird" on the guitar. Given the specifics of any given day, I might introduce myself in a variety of ways. That is, no doubt, true for you as well. But on our hardest days, it is helpful to remember who we are at our core. Our truest identity in this world is defined not by what we have accomplished, but by what God has done. God has claimed us. We are children of God, not because of the love that lives in our hearts but because of the love that lives in God's heart. By the mysteries of grace, we belong to God.

Philippians 1:3–11

[3]I thank my God every time I remember you, [4]constantly praying with joy in every one of my prayers for all of you, [5]because of your sharing in the gospel from the first day until now. [6]I am confident of this, that the one who began a good work among you will bring it to completion by the day of Jesus Christ. [7]It is right for me to think this way about all of you, because you hold me in your heart, for all of you share in God's grace with me, both in my imprisonment and in the defense and confirmation of the gospel. [8]For God is my witness, how I long for all of you with the compassion of Christ Jesus. [9]And this is my prayer, that your love may overflow more and more with knowledge and full insight [10]to help you to determine what is best, so that in the day of Christ you may be pure and blameless, [11]having produced the harvest of righteousness that comes through Jesus Christ for the glory and praise of God.

Thanks

Paul offers a prayer of thanksgiving for the church. Praying prayers of thanksgiving for the church may not be a common practice, but it is actually a good and helpful thing to do. This may be particularly helpful if you are a leader of the church and therefore know the ins and outs of church life. Sometimes, when we do not simply go to church but actually serve the church, we discover frustration. We see up close that the church is not always "doing justice, loving kindness, and walking humbly with God," but, rather, doing little that matters, loving gossip, and walking on each other. Sometimes the church majors in minors and confuses the color of the choir robes with something ultimately more important, like bearing witness to the promised day of God. It can be frustrating. Hang around the church long enough, and the church will disappoint you. If you are in a particularly challenging situation, maybe put this book down and read through Corinthians . . . That church was so messed up, it is bound to make you feel better about whatever is frustrating your life of faith at the moment. Or, better yet, offer a prayer of thanksgiving for the saints in your life. Paul says, I thank my God every time I remember you. I'm sure Paul didn't thank God for everything he remembered about them. But he never failed to remember that which gave him reason for gratitude. Gratitude is less a feeling and more a practice. But the practice and the feeling are connected. Practice gratitude enough, and in time you might actually feel grateful. For Paul, he says he practiced it every time he prayed.

Thanks for Sharing

The first thing for which Paul is thankful is that the Philippians share in the gospel (Phil 1:5). The sharing was in part very tangible. The church sent a friend, Epaphroditus, to support Paul during his imprisonment (Phil 4:18). Paul is also expressing gratitude for financial gifts he has received from the Philippian congregation (Phil 4:10, 14–16). But these gifts are an expression of something deeper. Sharing in the gospel is not sharing an idea but, rather, sharing a relationship. Paul declares that they belong to one another, and this sense of belonging is profound. Paul gives thanks because, as he says, "You hold me in your heart." This can also be translated, "I hold you in my heart" (Phil 1:7). The ambiguity in the language points to the confidence Paul has that their affection is mutual. When Paul prays, he does not pray that God would help him or cause the doors to the jail cell to swing open, like they did the time Paul and Silas were having a midnight hymn sing (Acts 16:26). No, he prays that their love not only for him but even more so for one another may increase (Phil 1:9).

Their love for one another is crucial. Paul Sampley says, "More than any other church represented in the corpus, the Philippians grew and matured in faith such that they were truly like [Paul] from early on in their relationship."[3] They are mature in faith (Phil 3:15). But the journey of faith never stops. Loving one another is never static but has to be chosen again and again each day.

When I was in college, I was hired as a choir director in a small rural Baptist church. I could not have been the best musician they had ever had, but they welcomed me like I had grown up in their family. My friends in

3. Sampley, "Reasoning from the Horizons," 121.

that church would sometimes speak of their faith in terms of their conversion. They would talk about the time Jesus came into their hearts. That was not familiar language for me. My tradition was more academic and would probably have been more comfortable speaking of Jesus coming into our thoughts. I come from a tradition that deeply values the stewardship of the mind. But I think both, head and heart, are too small. To describe Christian faith either way remains too individualistic. Faith is personal, that's for certain. But Christian faith is not private. Jesus does not come into our heads or into our hearts; Jesus comes into our relationships. That's where trust in Jesus Christ shows up—in how we treat one another. This is not just the way it should be; it is a given. It is not simply hard to be Christian by yourself; it is impossible to be Christian by yourself, because the place that Jesus abides is our relationships.

Paul's affection for the Philippians runs deep. He says, "I long for you with the compassion of Christ" (Phil 1:8). The Greek word translated as compassion is *splanchna,* which refers to emotion from the pit of your stomach, from your core. This word is sometimes used to describe the compassion Jesus has for individuals or crowds. It is a compassion that compels action. It is a yearning that requires sacrifice. Daniel Migliore says it this way: "Christian friendship is a participation in the compassionate love of God in Christ even to death on a cross. Christians are called to love God and neighbor not halfheartedly, or on certain occasions, or with a thousand reservations, but as God loves the world and as Paul says he loves the Philippians—'with the compassion of Christ.'"[4]

Bill was my friend, and for a season I was his pastor. His son Billy told me that Bill was in the Battle of the Bulge, but Bill never talked about that. Bill and Evelyn were high school sweethearts, but when the war came, he went into the service. When the war ended, he came home. They were married in the church and had a reception in the same fellowship hall where they had gathered for youth fellowship every Sunday night when they were in high school. Bill worked in insurance, Evelyn was a math teacher. They raised two children, both boys.

By the time I met Bill and Evelyn, they lived in a retirement community. He was in independent living, she was in memory care. Whenever I visited them, I would always find Bill in her room. He would tell her stories about a life she could no longer remember, about children she no longer recognized, and about a husband who had loved her from across the ocean

---

4. Migliore, *Philippians and Philemon,* 32.

and back. She appeared to delight in these stories, even if they struck her as the narrative of someone else altogether.

I stopped by one day. He was reading while she rested. My arrival awakened her. I introduced myself again. She said, "Nice to meet you." Then pointing to Bill, she said, "Have you met this nice man?" "Yes, I have," I said.

After we shared the same visit we always had, I took my exit. Bill followed me into the hall. I said, "Bill, I can only imagine how sad this is. Tell me, what keeps you coming? It is clear, she doesn't remember that you are the one who has loved her in plenty and in want, joy and sorrow, sickness and health all these years."

"Tom, I know she doesn't remember me," he said. "Dementia is the cruelest of conditions, as it robs her of her own life. I suppose it robs us both of her life. I don't come because she might remember me; I come because I can't forget her. I just can't stay away. It's the only place I know to be."

It's not easy and it may sound impossible, but sometimes we can love not halfheartedly or with reservations but with the compassion of Christ. I've seen it.

The grace of God ties us together. I think this is a reason that even from prison, Paul can be joyful, because not even prison can dissolve the bonds of love that he holds for and receives from the saints in Philippi. Paul has to face his imprisonment. No one can do his time for him. But he is not alone. No doubt he gives thanks to God that he is not alone.

Everyone will face the dark night of the soul, as some have named it, or the wilderness journey, as others describe it. When it comes to us, we have to walk our own walk. But we don't have to walk alone. If I understand the text, Paul is not only exhorting the Philippians to keep their love for him, but just as much, their love for one another. As saints and servants of Christ, they share a bond and a power that not even the likes of Caesar can destroy.

The End of the Story

In this prayer of thanksgiving, Paul does something typically Pauline. As he prays for the Philippians, he looks over their shoulder and off into the horizon. He says, "I am convinced that the one who began a good work in you will bring it to completion on the day of Jesus Christ" (Phil 1:6). This phrase—the day of Jesus Christ—is a reference to God's ultimate work of redemption. It's what Mark means by the kingdom of God. It's what Matthew means when he speaks of the kingdom of heaven. The day of Jesus

Christ is when the transformative work of God's love revealed in Christ is brought to completion. We don't live in that day now. No, far from it. But Paul trusts that God will be faithful. To profess this conviction from prison grants insight into the confidence that carries Paul even in difficult times. It is a confidence in the faithfulness of God.

In these few verses, we are handed a sketch of how Paul understands time. He speaks of the first day and of the day of Jesus Christ. The first day is the day the gospel was first preached and trusted in Philippi. The day of Jesus Christ is that eschatological day, the day the prophets promised, when justice will roll down like waters (Amos 5:24), the wolf shall live with the lamb (Isa 11:6), the law will be written on the heart (Jer 31:33), and the hungry are filled with good things (Luke 1:53). On that final day of ultimate redemption, all that has gone wrong will be made right, the new creation will be finished, and the whole of creation will be "lost in wonder, love and praise."[5]

This means that Paul, the Philippians, and the rest of us live in the in-between days. We live between the first day and the promised day of Jesus Christ. While living in between, we share in the gospel. Again, sharing in the gospel is not an idea, a doctrine, or a program. To share in the gospel is to share in a community shaped by the love of Christ. The fact that Paul is in prison and still points to the day of Christ Jesus makes one thing clear: in these in-between days, God will not keep you from trouble. Faith provides no sanctuary from suffering; indeed, Paul's current suffering is a direct result of his trust in Jesus Christ. God will not keep you from trouble, but God will bring you through.

He tells the Philippians, I can see the good that God has already done in you, by the way you love one another and how you have loved me. I can see the love of Christ in your relationships, but God is not finished with you yet. That good work will be brought to completion.

There is a very practical but important practice revealed here. Paul looks for the good and points it out. The Philippian church was faithful, but they weren't perfect. Paul will have some things to say about ways their love for one another might increase. And yet he tells them, I see the good in you.

I received a call to join a congregation in ministry and serve as their pastor. I was excited, because, as I looked at them, I saw innovative mission. I saw deep care for one another. I saw a hunger to worship God with honesty. It took me a while to recognize that I saw what many of them could no longer see. This congregation had a rich history of courageous

---

5. Wesley, "Love Divine."

ministry, but at the time of my arrival, because of some things they could control and many they couldn't, they felt their most recent days had not been their best. They were discouraged. They were defeated. They weren't wrong. There were ways that their love for God and one another needed to grow. Growing in that shared love is just what started to happen, as together we began to see the good that God was already doing among us. Paul is being a good pastoral mentor here: look for the good. It is there in the good that we witness the fingerprints of God in the church.

But then Paul says, that good, which is obviously incomplete, will be brought to completion on the promised day of Jesus Christ. Pointing out the good that God has done among them does not create a false sense of having arrived. No, quite the opposite. Identifying what God has done among them pushes the imagination of who they can be as a community of saints in Christ. The future is not defined by the dreams we might have. Our dreams are often shaped by skepticism informed by our own failings. But Paul knows the future is defined not by the dreams we might imagine but by the dreams God refuses to relinquish. Paul speaks of the completion of God's dreams for us with a confidence that reason itself might question. But once you have traveled to the end of what reason might support, there is still a truth that love has learned to trust. The way we are with one another now is incomplete, we are not home yet, and the promised day of Christ has yet to arrive in all its fullness. But in Christ, we get a glimpse of that day. The promised day of Christ becomes our North Star, inviting us to let that day shape our present. In faith, we trust the day of Christ—a day we have yet to see—but nevertheless the day on which we base our lives.

In 1965, Admiral Jim Stockdale was shot down over Vietnam. For eight years, he was held as a prisoner of war. He was the highest ranking military officer in the so-called Hanoi Hilton. He was tortured over twenty times. Yet, he still devised ways to comfort and lead others. He was asked once, "Over all those years, how did you deal with it all?" Admiral Stockdale said, "I never lost faith in the end of the story. I never doubted not only that I would get out, but also that I would prevail in the end and turn the experience into the defining event of my life."[6]

The end of the story of which he speaks is the faithfulness of the United States military and the commitment to leave no soldier behind. He was also asked, "Who didn't make it out?" He responded, "The optimists. They were the ones who said, 'We will be out by Christmas.' Christmas would come,

6. Collins, Good to Great, 85.

and Christmas would go. Then they'd say, 'We will be out by Easter.' And Easter would come, and Easter would go. And then Thanksgiving, and then it would be Christmas again. And they died of a broken heart."[7]

Paul tells us to remember the end of the story. We are part of a story that began on the first day, when the love of God imagined the world into being. It is a story where that same creative love was revealed with clarity and compassion in the life of the Jewish rabbi named Jesus, who humbled himself to give everything he had for a world God loves. When it looked like all might be lost, he was raised in glory. It is a story told through the rich history of saints, who in both beauty and brokenness have borne witness to this holy love. The love of God proclaimed in this story is a love that will never let us go. So ours is a story of promise that the good in us and in the world will be brought to completion. It's not a story that is based in optimism, because we are not the writers of this story. It is a story that relies on the conviction that God is faithful. It is a story you can trust every day, even on hard days. Let your trust in this holy story shape your choices and define your relationships. Let your trust in this story provide the lens through which you see the contours of your own life, as well as the world. Trust that life's circumstances do not determine the promises of God, but, rather, the promises of God lead us through life circumstances. Trust that story like you trust gravity, and, even on the hardest days, joy can come to you.

7. Collins, *Good to Great*, 85.

CHAPTER 2

This Could Be Us

CANCER AGAIN. CANCER IS no respecter of persons. It will attack anyone, and when it does, it doesn't just attack the person, it attacks everyone who loves that person. This time it was Tom. He was my friend. We looked nothing alike, but we did share the same name, and he was about my age, which was much too young to be that sick. His beautiful children were heartbroken as they watched his decline. His wife of over twenty years was lost. "I don't even know where he got the cars serviced," she said. "He just took care of those kinds of things. I don't want to bother him with trivial things like that now, but what am I going to do?" The enormity of grief can never be expressed in totality, so it comes out in smaller losses, like the helplessness of getting a car serviced. I sat by his bedside. It was one of those hospital beds they can set up in your home. He chose his living room to do his dying in. We read "I go to prepare a place for you" and "nothing separates us from the love of God." I asked him what he thought about heaven. "It will be beautiful," he said. But then he wondered, "Will I be lonely there without Julie? I don't guess it can be heaven if you are lonely." He laughed. But then he said, "I can't imagine being without her and not being lonely. I guess God still has some work to do with me."

Here's the truth that I wish were not the truth. I left his living room a little shell-shocked. It was not the conversation about heaven that unsettled me. While I have grown more and more humble in my understanding of the nature of heaven, I have grown more and more confident in my trust that, in the end, there is only God. I trust that God is love. I have learned from my own life that one thing love does very poorly is to let go. That's why grief is so hard; we just aren't wired to let go of those we love. We love with a love that holds on, because the God who created us loves just that way. I know nothing about what we will look like in heaven, or if there is peach cobbler like my grandmother used to make, or if I will be able to play guitar like Eric Clapton; but I do trust that the love of God simply refuses to let go of us. And yet, as I left Tom after what I sensed was our last visit, and as I crossed his front lawn, my own thoughts were, "Oh God, this could be me. I could already have cancer and not even know it yet. This could be me."

Philippians 1:12–13

¹²I want you to know, beloved, that what has happened to me has actually helped to spread the gospel, ¹³so that it has become known throughout the whole imperial guard and to everyone else that my imprisonment is for Christ.

But, Paul, How Are You?

One of the things about reading someone else's mail is we join the conversation midstream. There are previous experiences and earlier conversations that create a background to the letter that we read now. But epistles have no footnotes. We aren't clued into those moments when Paul is assuming, "Hey, guys, remember when we talked about such and such before? Well, here's what I have to say about that now." This is our situation with this letter. This letter is not the beginning of a conversation but, rather, an ongoing conversation we are dropping into.

So, an important step in interpreting the letter is to try to ascertain what may be going on in the congregation that Paul is addressing. It's like trying to discern the other side of the phone call when you hear only one side. The letter is not some abstract theological treatise that Paul is writing for an unspecified public. He is writing to reflect on particular circumstances that have occurred and to respond to specific questions that have emerged in Philippi. But what are those questions?

If I understand the text, a significant issue Paul wishes to address is the Philippians' concern for their friend and pastor. Their first question is, "Paul, are you okay?" The congregation has learned that Paul is in prison and, naturally, they are concerned for him. They sent Epaphroditus to care for Paul, but Epaphroditus grew ill, only increasing the concerns in Philippi. They want to know how Paul is faring. Is he eating well? Is the cell cold? Is he being mistreated? Are the nights long? Is he lonely or afraid? They are eager to hear a word from their pastor and friend: "Paul, tell us, how are you?"

Beloved

There would be many reasons that the church might be concerned for Paul. The circumstances of prison could be harsh. But more than that, Paul was in prison because of his faith. That's a shot across the bow for all who confess that Jesus, not Caesar, is Lord—including the saints in Philippi. No one wants prison to be a major stop along one's spiritual journey.

Paul is grateful for their care, as they are a source of strength for him. We see this as Paul uses a word that is common in Scripture but one that should not be taken for granted. He calls them beloved. The Greek term is *adelphoi,* which is literally translated as brothers. The NRSV and others opt for a more inclusive beloved, which I appreciate. But brothers and sisters might be a better option, because it retains the sense that Paul sees the Philippians as family. This is a family whom Caesar has divided.

My friend Arlin teaches a poetry class in a nearby correctional facility. The inmates with whom he works are pretty amazing poets. They write poems about life in and out of incarceration. One of the realities of prison life, separated from loved ones, is an inescapable loneliness. So many of these poets on the inside have been forgotten by those on the outside. Many of them tell of mothers or children or even spouses who make visits for a while, but then the visits spread out, until they just stop. The inmates are left to construct community among the busted, beleaguered, and abandoned inmate population. To be cut off from love is lonely. It shows up in their poems.

Got Class
New kid
never one school
skipping, smoking, coping
it's my world, my insanity
outcast.[1]

---

1. North, "Got Class."

Outcast. Ignored. Forgotten. Prison is lonely. It is clear Paul cherished contact with those he called beloved (Phil 1:12). They are a lifeline for him, while this man of seemingly endless energy passes time locked up. Of course, you don't have to be in prison to be lonely. We live in a very lonely culture. We can be surrounded by people and still be lonely.

I think about the kids sitting in class, looking around at everyone there, and the presence of all those other students only intensifies the feeling of loneliness. Or a grandmother, new to her retirement community, with a collection of 5x7's of beautiful, well-posed grandchildren on top of the TV, and down the hall is a dining room full of strangers. Or you pass dozens of people in the office hallway every day. "How are you? Fine, thanks, you?" But no one can stop long enough to know the stress that every heart carries.

Technology is a factor in contemporary American loneliness. Our means of connection often creates contact with limited intimacy. "In a world consumed by ever more novel modes of socializing, we have less and less actual social society. We live in an accelerating contradiction: the more connected we become, the lonelier we are."[2] Sherry Turkel teaches computer culture at MIT. In her book *Alone Together,* she writes, "These days, insecure in our relationships and anxious about intimacy, we look to technology for ways to be in relationships and protect ourselves from them at the same time . . . . The ties we form through the Internet are not, in the end, the ties that bind. But they are the ties that preoccupy."[3] Turkel is a bit harsh here. But the challenge with digital connection is that it is ultimately incomplete. Our whole self never shows up online. After a year of posting worship videos on the church's website as the pandemic has chased us from one another, it is common to hear, "I love the services online, but it's not the same as in person." Amen. When we love one another, we long to be together.

Being physically cut off from his congregations is something that Paul never took lightly. He urges Philemon to prepare a room, for he wants to come and visit (Phlm 24). He tells the Corinthians, "I don't wish to see you just in passing, for I hope to spend some time with you" (1 Cor 16:7). In a tender moment, Second Timothy records Paul's dying request: Timothy, "do your best to come to me soon" (2 Tim 4:9). And here, Paul speaks of a communion that is deeper than geographical proximity. They are family. When he cannot be with them, naming and claiming the bond between Paul and his beloved congregation is a source of strength for Paul. The

2. Marche, "Is Facebook Making Us Lonely," para 4.

3. Turkel, as cited in Marche, "Is Facebook Making Us Lonely," para 37.

Philippians miss Paul, and he yearns for them (Phil 1:8). Paul expresses a profound sense of gratitude for the Philippians, because they have been faithful friends. They have reminded Paul that he might be by himself, but he is not alone, for together they are family. They are beloved.

Perhaps Paul is hoping the familial bond will strengthen the Philippians as well.

For Christ: The Reality of Othering

Paul acknowledges that he is imprisoned for Christ. It is his faith that has created this circumstance or, more accurately, the way the powers of society respond to his faith that has landed him in jail. Paul is in prison because he has been *othered*. Followers of Jesus, in Paul's day, had very little social status. More than that, many saw the Christian faith as strange. They engaged in strange worship practices and even allowed men and women, slaves and free, to all eat at the same table. Many, and many with power, looked at Christians not only as strange but perhaps even dangerous. When folks with power see others as strange or dangerous, it's seldom good for those who are seen this way.

When someone seems strange, we don't think of him or her as being like us. It is easy for those deemed not like us to become othered. We see this in our own lives and in our own culture all the time.

Bryan Stevenson was driving south of Atlanta through rural farmlands to reach the Georgia Diagnostic and Classification Center, informally known as Jackson. At the time, Stevenson was a law student at Harvard Law School and an intern with the Southern Prisoners Defense Committee. The Diagnostic and Classification Center sounds like a medical center, but it is the largest prison in the state of Georgia. It is where men awaiting lethal injection are incarcerated.

Stevenson arrived to visit an inmate named Henry. By the time the visit had concluded, Stevenson's life work was launched. He would spend his life following Jesus's commandment to set the prisoners free. When setting them free is not the just pursuit, he ensures they have adequate legal counsel. At other times, he simply makes sure that they know they haven't been forgotten. Stevenson writes:

> When I first went to death row in December 1983, America was in the early stages of a radical transformation that would turn us into an unprecedentedly harsh and punitive nation and result in

mass imprisonment that has no historical parallel. Today we have the highest rate of incarceration in the world. The prison population has increased from 300,000 people in the early 1970's to 2.3 million people today . . . . One in every fifteen people born in the United States in 2001 is expected to go to jail or prison; one in every three black male babies born in this century is expected to be incarcerated.[4]

As Stevenson identifies, the racial makeup of prisons never reflects the racial makeup of society as a whole. For people of color, their incarceration rates far exceeds their percentage of the overall population. There are economic reasons that contribute to this. There are reasons found in the persistent realities of systemic racism. But there are also reasons as ancient as the apostle Paul.

A universal human struggle is the difficulty we often have in seeing the full humanity of someone we judge as different from us. The difference can be race. It can be economic status. It can be culture. It can be the fact that another talks with speech patterns that are not like the folks back home. I live in the metropolitan area of Kansas City. One of the rare qualities of my home city is the fact that it straddles the state line. The metropolitan area is in both Kansas and Missouri (pronounce that either way you like . . . Missouree or Missourah). I came to Kansas City from the South. Given that I'm not a native to the area, I noticed right away that folks sometimes talk about "those folks" from the other side of the state line as if they are strangers in a strange land and not like us. It's usually pretty comical, given they might live three blocks apart and all shop in the same stores, attend the same church, and root for the same teams. It can be comical, until it's not. To speak simply about it, the human temptation is to categorize people as us and others. This is a universal human reality: as soon as my mind registers that that person is not like me, it becomes harder to see the full humanity of the other person.

Dr. Jennifer Eberhardt, a psychology professor at Stanford, explains the mental mechanics of othering or bias. She explains our brains are wired to use the tool of categorization. We categorize food, furniture, and animals, for example. These categories hold information but also feelings, beliefs, and associations. If you see a cat, you don't have to know the particular cat to know the category. Therefore, you might immediately want to take the cat home, if you are the type to want cats in your home. If it is the kind of

4. Stevenson, *Just Mercy*, 15.

cat who would eat you for dinner, you leave it in the zoo. You don't need to know the particular animal to know all of this, because your brain knows the category.

We categorize people, too. Muslims and Catholics. Rich and poor. Educated and not. The history of the United States has been a long story of categorization by race. It is our most common practice of othering. Dr. Eberhardt says,

> Whether good or bad, whether justified or unjustified, our beliefs and attitudes can become so strongly associated with the category that they are automatically triggered, affecting our behavior and decision making. So, for example, simply seeing a black person can automatically bring to mind a host of associations that we have picked up from society: this person is a good athlete, this person doesn't do well in school, this person is poor, this person dances well, this person lives in a black neighborhood, this person should be feared. The process of making these connections is called bias. It can happen unintentionally. It can happen unconsciously. It can happen effortlessly. And it can happen in a matter of milliseconds. These associations take hold of us no matter our values, no matter our conscious beliefs, no matter what kind of person we wish to be in the world.[5]

When it is harder to see the full humanity of another, it is easier to treat him or her as lesser. It is easier to pass by on the other side or lock the person up and throw away the key.

Michelle Alexander has studied mass incarceration in America, and she writes: "Once you're labeled a felon, the old forms of discrimination—employment discrimination, housing discrimination, denial of the right to vote, denial of educational opportunity, denial of food stamps and other public benefits, and exclusion from jury service—are suddenly legal. As a criminal, you have scarcely more rights, and arguably less respect, than a black man living in Alabama at the height of Jim Crow. We have not ended racial caste in America; we have merely redesigned it."[6]

Don't let me mislead. I am not suggesting that Paul's imprisonment was racially motivated. It wasn't. I am saying that racism is part of the American story of incarceration. I am also saying there is a connection between the American circumstance and Paul's struggle. The connection is not racism,

5. Eberhardt, *Biased*, 31–32.
6. Alexander, *New Jim Crow*, 2.

but a more generic othering. Racism is a specific expression of othering but not the only one. Paul was an evangelist for a faith that was viewed with suspicion by civil authorities. He writes, my imprisonment is for Christ. As a Christian in his day, he was viewed as other and therefore lesser.

The tables would turn and turn quickly. Emperor Constantine would bless the Christian faith, bringing a great reversal, lifting Christians from the prisons of powerlessness to the thrones of cultural muscle. Sadly, the move would often prove painful, even dangerous, for non-Christians over the centuries, as with self-righteous certainty, the church deemed a variety of heathens to be others who are not like us. At times, the consequences have been deadly.

Yet what Paul knew and what the Philippians feared was that their faith put them at risk with the powers that be. Their devotion to Jesus Christ meant they were not part of the mainstream. They were the strange eaters of body and blood. They seldom existed without opponents and, at times, powerful opponents. By the time Rome was feeding Christians to the lions, it is fair to say, followers of Jesus had lost the status of being seen as human. Paul's crime was less that he broke the law and more that he was deemed less than. But Paul knows, in Christ, he is beloved.

I Want You to Know

In the winter of 1945, U.S. serviceman Jack Utech wrote a letter to his parents from "somewhere in the Philippines." He said, "At this moment I am thinking very much of home. It is curious how far back the mind reaches when separation and solitude are forced upon a [person]. Memories must be God's recompense for pressing times." And then he wrote, "I regret I described the air raids so vividly in a recent letter. I do not want to open for mother a new channel for anxiety."[7]

Paul writes not simply to let the Philippians know how he is doing. He writes to address their anxiety. The Philippians are concerned about how the apostle is faring, but they are concerned for themselves as well. For no doubt, when they learned how the servant of Christ is treated in Caesar's world, they knew they could share the same fate. They had to also be thinking, "Oh God, this could be us."

So, Paul tells them, "I want you to know, beloved, that what has happened to me has actually helped to spread the gospel" (Phil 1:12–13).

7. Utech, "Letter from the Philippines," 97.

But, Paul, how are you?

"I want you to know that what has happened to me has actually helped to spread the gospel."

But, Paul, are you being mistreated?

"I want you to know . . ."

If I understand the text, this is Paul's answer to their concern for his well-being. Paul is teaching them, if you want to know how things are with me, then you need to know how things are with the gospel. Toward that end, because I am in this prison, the guards know that I have faith in Jesus Christ.

Paul is telling us how his life is defined. He is not defined by what the Romans have done to him. He is defined by what God has done for him through Christ. Meaning in his daily life is rooted in something much larger than the circumstances of his day. Paul understands that he is participating in God's work of redemption in the world. He is not seeing this in a boastful or arrogant manner but, rather, as the truth that gives him peace and even joy. He knows prison can't change his calling or his ability to bear witness to Christ. It doesn't matter where he is or what the circumstances might be; the opportunity to live as a servant of Christ is always available. So, the circumstances of his life do not determine his faith; his faith determines how he navigates the circumstances of his life. He may be in Caesar's prison, but he is Christ's servant, and it is that calling and that purpose that gives his life meaning and joy.

Bryan Stevenson sat down on a seat bolted to the floor across from Henry, the death row inmate he had driven from Atlanta to see. Stevenson was nervous, as he had little good news to share. He told Henry that they still were working to find him an attorney, and that Stevenson himself was just an intern, still a law student. The best news he had to share hardly seemed like good news at all: they did not expect that Henry would be executed within the year. Henry thanked him. Then the guard stated that it was time to go back to his cell. The guard was aggressive. At one point, as the guard shoved him toward the exit, Henry stopped lifted his head and began to sing in a tremendous baritone voice.

> I'm pressing on the upward way,
> New heights I'm gaining ev'ry day;
> Still praying as I'm onward bound,
> "Lord, plant my feet on higher ground."

Brian said he recognized the song from church. It was a gift. He writes, "I had no right to expect anything from a condemned man on death row.

Yet he gave me an astonishing measure of his humanity. In that moment, Henry altered something in my understanding of human potential, redemption and hopefulness."[8]

> Lord, lift me up, and let me stand
> By faith, on heaven's tableland;
> A higher plane than I have found,
> Lord, plant my feet on higher ground.

Just as Henry, from the inside, ministered to Brian on the outside, Paul ministers to the Philippians. He writes to say, if the gospel is lived—in here or out there—then we will be fine.

Secondly, did you notice, he doesn't say the guards have faith in Christ. He just says they know that Paul has faith in Christ. This is so important. For much of my life, I assumed that it was my job to encourage those around me to be Christian. That's not a bad thing, but it is definitely a secondary thing. Paul understands that his job is not to make his neighbor a Christian; his job is to be Christian to his neighbor. If they can see his trust in Christ, that is enough. I don't think when the promised day of Christ finally comes, Jesus is going to ask me why my neighbor isn't a Christian. Jesus will just want to know if I was Christian to my neighbor. The only life you can be Christian with is your own. Your neighbors may not believe in Jesus Christ themselves, but it will be pleasing to God if they can see that you do.

Philippians 1:14–18a

[14]and most of the brothers and sisters, having been made confident in the Lord by my imprisonment, dare to speak the word with greater boldness and without fear.
[15]Some proclaim Christ from envy and rivalry, but others from goodwill. [16]These proclaim Christ out of love, knowing that I have been put here for the defense of the gospel; [17]the others proclaim Christ out of selfish ambition, not sincerely but intending to increase my suffering in my imprisonment. [18]What does it matter? Just this, that Christ is proclaimed in every way, whether out of false motives or true; and in that I rejoice.

---

8. Stevenson, *Just Mercy*, 12. Cited: "I'm Pressing on the Upward Way (Higher Ground)," by Johnson Oatman Jr.

Would I Meet People Like Jesus?

Because Paul is in prison, there are other preachers who are bolder now. Paul knows they have various reasons and motivations for their preaching, but he clearly celebrates that the word is being proclaimed, even by less than perfect vessels. Paul states that some do this from good motives and some from poor motives. He rejoices either way, as long as they proclaim Jesus Christ.

We must interpret this with care. It would be a mistake to read this and assume that motives are irrelevant in life. That would not be a wise interpretation of this passage. Motives matter. But the truth is, our motives are never pure. Often, motives exist in conflict with each other. To be human is to live with a fragmented heart.

My daughter graduated from high school, and that's when it hit me: she would be leaving for college in the fall. I was a mess. I expected to grieve, but I didn't expect it to be as difficult as it was. When the day finally came, her mother, brother, and I dropped her off in the middle of Iowa. God did not create fathers to leave their little girls in Iowa. I cried the entire three-hour trip home. The irony is that my daughter was doing exactly what I wanted her to do. It would have been much worse if she had come down to the breakfast table that morning and said, "Dad, I have been thinking it over, and I have decided I'm not going to college. I've decided I'm just going to live here with you guys." In going to college, she was doing exactly what I wanted her to do. I just didn't want what I wanted. That makes me a bit hard to please, I admit. At times, a fragmented heart is impossible to escape. We want conflicting things at the same time. Motivations are never pure.

When it comes to the gospel, none of us can claim that we live purely. All of us stumble. Or, to use the language more common in our culture, there is some hypocrisy in all of us. We don't live up to our greatest ideals all the time.

Mark Labberton is a pastor and seminary president. One Sunday, he noticed a young adult at worship. This guy had not been there before, so Mark struck up a conversation with him. He learned he was a grad student at the University of California. Mark asked him, "What brings you to this church?" He said he had recently been asking some significant questions about his life, and that had led him to church. I've been to a number of churches, and they talk a lot about Jesus and about the world. I'm not really sure what I'm looking for, but "here's what I want to know: if I hang out at your church, will I meet people who are actually *like* Jesus?"[9]

If someone asked you that question, what would you say? The question makes me a little uncomfortable, because I know there is a big gap between the life I live and the life of Jesus. The essence of Christ is love—a consistent, persistent, transformative love. At times, I've seen love like that in the church. I've experienced that kind of love in the community of faith. But I also know that love like that is not a given in the church, and sometimes we fall short. Way short!

My wife and I were returning from a trip to Scotland. We flew across the Atlantic, first landing in Philadelphia. From there we caught a plane to Chicago, where we hoped to catch our final flight to Kansas City. But the weather, which had been bad all day, grew worse. After having been awake for twenty-seven hours and having multiple flights delayed, we were finally told that our flight was cancelled. There would be no flight to Kansas City until the next day. We were stuck in Chicago for the night. We found a room at a nearby hotel and hailed a cab. It was the worst cab ride in the history of transportation. The windshield defroster didn't work, so the driver kept his window down. This allowed the rain and some snow to fly unimpeded upon us in the back seat. In broken English, he asked me to use my phone for directions to the hotel. The Garmin in the cab wasn't working. It was one o'clock in the morning, and I was not overly kind. I was not mean. I was just what my family describes as short. I said, "I'm not supposed to be telling you how to get there, you are supposed to get us there. That's your job. Now, turn right at the next light."

When we arrived at our hotel, my wife Carol said to me, "Tom, what do you think that guy's life is like?" From his language, it was clear he hadn't been in the country long. His cab was in bad shape, and he was driving the midnight shift, so obviously he was new to his job. If he was like some other immigrants we have known, he likely spends his day emptying trashcans at a nursing home or working a loading dock, and he is spending his nights driving this broken-down cab. She said, "It looks like he is doing everything he can to make it, and he is barely holding on. The least you could do is be kind."

I was ashamed. I was also grateful that he didn't know I was a pastor. This immigrant, from somewhere in Africa, very well may have been a Christian himself, and I did not treat him with kindness. There was a moment when I could have chosen to live a little more like Jesus, but I failed.

9. Labberton, *Called*, 26.

I know that the essential nature of Jesus is love—a persistent, consistent, transformative love that dwells in his marrow, his *splanchna*. Yet, for a midnight ride in Chicago, I gave no indication that I trusted that love, for it failed to show up in me. Paul says the guards know he is in prison for Christ; but there was no way for the cab driver to know I was a Christian.

"If I hang out at your church, will I meet people who are like Jesus?"

There is always a gap between the person we know we are supposed to be and the person we are in the moment. We are not like Jesus at all. But then, sometimes, we are. What Paul wants us to do is lean into that bold calling and not give up. We are to trust that the love of God not only claims us but shows up in us, trust that the love of Christ shows up in our relationships so that even the guards know who we are and whose we are.

One young adult asked Mark Labberton, "Will I meet people like Jesus here?" Mark had a variety of thoughts in response to that question. I do, too. But, eventually, here is what I would say, "Yes. Yes, you would. Of course, to see Christ in one another, we have to look closely, because the folks in church are never perfect. But the truth is, the closest I have ever come to knowing Jesus is in the community of faith. For it is among the beautiful and broken people of God that I have known forgiveness that is real and welcome that is genuine. It is among the beautiful and broken people of God that I have known generosity and sacrificial love. It is among the fragmented and fragile people of God that I have seen a bold hope and a desire to choose the high road, even when we are afraid. I think the most likely place you will see Jesus is in the community of the church."

You may greet that statement with skepticism, and I wouldn't blame you. Because it is also true that the church is a mess at times. The litany of church failings is significant, and failure never skips a generation. Throughout history, the church has been on the wrong side of so many issues, it is hard to keep track. But that is only part of the story. The other part of the story is that sometimes the love of God shows up in spite of our sin, and sometimes that love sculpts our speech and our actions in a way that, if you look closely enough, you might see a glimpse of the love that has claimed us shining through the cracks of our discipleship. Paul trusts that, and he exhorts us to trust it as well.

I stood in the sanctuary of Westminster Presbyterian Church in Charleston, South Carolina, on a sweltering August day. The temperature was hot enough to melt your hair. The sanctuary was filled with family and friends. I was wearing a rented tux and had come to say my wedding vows.

As you know, the wedding vows are pretty bold promises. We promise to be loving. It's not a promise of what we will feel; it's a promise of how we will treat each other. Understood theologically, love shows up not simply in our emotions, but in our choices. It is patient and kind, not envious or boastful or arrogant or rude. To love is to live for the good of another, as best as you are able.

"I, Tom, promise to be loving and faithful." I said it just that way. I suppose in full transparency, I could have qualified it a bit. I promise to be loving, and I know love requires kindness, but I'm not always kind. Sometimes I am short. So, should we put an asterisk by love just to avoid hypocrisy? No, it doesn't work that way. Was I hypocritical in my marriage vow? Yes, in part, I suppose I was. Even in marriage, we sometimes live with a fragmented heart. But the response to that hypocrisy is not to reduce the bold promise to something that we can manage easily. It's not faithful to crank down the expectation to fit our comfort level. No, instead we lean boldly into the best we can offer.

I think that is what Paul is talking about. The proclaimers of the gospel were a mixed bag. Their motives were not pure. Ours never are either. But when we do our best, we make our offering, we tell our truth, and then trust that the power of the risen Christ can use the imperfect to do gospel work.

"If I hang out at your church, will I meet people who are like Jesus?"

Yes. They are also sinners. But their failings do not define them, just like your failings do not define you. Ultimately, none of us is defined by the worst in us, but by the best in God. So, the truth is, every one of these sinners is also a saint. Because Christ is love, and love is a power, we look at the way he lived and with a humble hope confess, "Oh God, thanks be to God, that could be us."

CHAPTER 3

Some Days Are Like That

FOR THE PAST SEVENTEEN years, I have had the privilege to serve the congregation of the Village Presbyterian Church in a suburb of Kansas City. In 1947, Rev. Bob Meneilly, fresh from seminary, wanted to serve as a missionary to China, but China closed to missionary activity. So Rev. Meneilly found himself in a place called Prairie Village, Kansas, which at the time was more prairie than village. He came to organize a new church. After two years of his walking the neighborhoods and knocking on doors, the Village Church was chartered in 1949. For forty-seven years, Dr. Bob, as he is known, served as the church's pastor and did so in a singular fashion. He served tirelessly and with a joyful spirit. A visit or phone call never ends without his saying, "Be of good cheer." These same words conclude his letters, as well as the message on his voice mail. (I think he still has an old answering machine.) His ministry faced challenging times, as he was vocal about his support of civil rights, his opposition to the Vietnam War, and his commitment to treat all of God's children as just that—God's children. Not everyone supported him, but it was hard not to love him, because even in those difficult times, he was a man of good cheer. Today, in his nineties, he is still that way, and his spirit is magnetic, drawing people to him. In my community, if you say, "Be of good cheer," a few folks may recognize these words as a saying of Jesus, but many will think first of Dr. Bob. "Be of good cheer" is found in John 16:33. Paul never read the Gospel of John, but if he had, I think Paul would have liked that verse very much.

Philippians 1:18b-20

Yes, and I will continue to rejoice, [19]for I know that through your prayers and the help of the Spirit of Jesus Christ this will turn out for my deliverance. [20]It is my eager expectation and hope that I will not be put to shame in any way, but that by my speaking with all boldness, Christ will be exalted now as always in my body, whether by life or by death.

Some Days Are Like That

I imagine the situation this way, and that's all it is—imagination. I see the old servant of Christ, in a dark, damp cell. Not much light, so he squints as he reads over his words one last time. He wants to make sure they are right before he sends them as a lifeline to an anxious congregation in Philippi. Like any preacher, he wants the words to be true, and he wants them to be honest.

For Paul, the honest words are, "I will continue to rejoice." When was the last time you said, "I will rejoice"? Rejoice is not a word that is common in our culture. If we do have moments of rejoicing, even seasons of rejoicing, they come on the good days when the college acceptance letter arrives, or the job offer comes through, or the home test reads pregnant, or the person your child chooses to marry appears to be a fine human being. These are moments when we rejoice. But these words are not expected from jail. Who would blame Paul if his words were filled with regret and sorrow?

There is another letter (most doubt it was actually written by Paul) where Paul sounds needier. Again, from prison he writes, "Do your best to come to me before winter" (2 Tim 4:21). In that moment, the bold and brash apostle sounds like any one of us who needs a friend. Joy seems to have slipped his grasp. But in the Philippian letter, his mind is clear, his heart is full, and his spirit strong: I will continue to rejoice.

I want to be like Paul, but fear I'm more like a kid named Alexander. I met him in a book I used to read to my children. Alexander says, "I went to sleep with gum in my mouth and now there's gum in my hair and when I got out of bed this morning I tripped on the skateboard and by mistake I dropped my sweater in the sink while the water was running and I could tell it was going to be a terrible, horrible, no good, very bad day."[1]

1. Viorst, *Alexander,* first line.

Alexander's day starts off terrible and gets worse. But his mother is there to offer words of compassion and wisdom. She doesn't say, "Don't worry, my child, all will be well." No, when Alexander complains that he's having a "terrible, horrible, no good very bad day," she says, "Some days are like that."[2]

Yes, they are. We all know days like that. Actually, if you haven't had a terrible, horrible, no good, very bad day, be patient, you will.

Ben and Carol Weir were missionaries for thirty years. In 1984, while serving in Beirut, Ben was taken hostage. He was held in captivity for sixteen months. Most of that time, he was kept in isolation. He tells of the time, after many months alone, he was allowed to be with another hostage, Father Martin Jenco. Father Jenco had also been in isolation for months. They were suspicious as to why their captors would allow them to be together. Why the change? They whispered to one another. They cried. Human connection after so many, many months alone was a precious gift. After months of being alone with their thoughts, ordinary conversation was grace.

Then Ben spotted something in the corner of the room that looked suspicious to him. "I think this room is bugged," he said. They now assumed their captors put them together hoping their conversation would reveal some tidbit of information that their captors would find valuable. Father Jenco reached for the bugging device. But it wasn't a bug; it turned out to be a solid air freshener. Then Ben described what happened next: "We laughed and laughed over my paranoia. My sides were hurting. I had not really laughed in fourteen months! I had cried, and I had occasionally smiled to myself, but I had not laughed. Now we joined in laughter, one of God's most incredible gifts."[3]

I will continue to rejoice. When is the last time you said that? It's worth thinking about. There is a life-giving healing in laughter, in joy. Joy is not the same thing as laughter or even happiness. But they are cousins. Of this family of human dispositions, joy is the most encompassing, the deepest one. Happiness is often tied to a favorable circumstance in life. But joy, as Paul demonstrates, can rise above circumstances that are anything but favorable. Joy is rooted in the confidence that the disappointments of life are not evidence that God has abandoned us. Joy is the fruit that results from trusting the spirit of Christ will work for our deliverance, as Paul says.

2. Viorst, *Alexander,* last line.
3. Weir et al., *Hostage Bound, Hostage Free,* 149.

Perhaps joy is the first taste of that deliverance. Happiness is something that finds us; it comes to us carried by the blessings of ordinary time. But joy is both at the same time, a gift as well as something that is pursued. Joy is both a grace and a discipline that demands courage. David Whyte has said, joy is "the dropping away of the anxious worried self . . . like a thankful death" and embracing of "a deep form of love."[4] Joy, as an expression of love, is a relational disposition; it connects, because it is rooted less in the circumstances of my life and more in the certain hope that I belong to the ultimate and defining love in the world. And by the grace of God, some days are like that.

In 1913, President Theodore Roosevelt set out with only a handful of men to explore an ink-black thousand-mile-long tributary of the Amazon called the River of Doubt. The river snaked its way through uncharted regions of the Brazilian rainforest. The risks of this journey were significant, and Roosevelt almost lost his life, which may have been the point. This was a quest. In 1912, Roosevelt left the Republican Party. In a hastily pulled together third party, he ran for president for an unprecedented third term. He took "Onward, Christian Soldiers" as his marching song and told his supporters they were facing Armageddon. The race did not go well for him. He was crushed in a three-way race which was won by the Democratic candidate, Woodrow Wilson. Failure was not something to which the old "Bull Moose" was accustomed. In January, Wilson was sworn in as president, and that autumn, Roosevelt, fearing the failure would define him, set out to chart the River of Doubt. To a family friend, Roosevelt said, "You don't know how lonely it is for a man to be rejected by his own kind."[5]

Sometimes life can throw us down our own river of doubt. Given the circumstances, it would be reasonable for Paul to find his spirit on a similar uncharted, meandering way. But Paul's words are not words of grief or anger or disappointment, and they certainly are not words of doubt. Paul says, "I will continue to rejoice." The fact that Paul says this from prison is one of the reasons the church has not been able to let go of this letter.

In spite of being shipwrecked, beaten, snakebitten, belittled, and now imprisoned, all because of his faith, Paul knows that joy is the courageous trust that the love of God is reliable. Teddy Roosevelt and Alexander show us what we already know: it's more common to be discouraged on your worst days. In no way do I condemn that response. Rejoicing is not my

4. Whyte, *Consolations*, 128.
5. Millard, *River of Doubt*, 14.

go-to on most days. And yet, I find myself drawn, like filings to a magnet, by the witness of the apostle. Maybe he had already lived through more than a few days of complaining. Maybe he wrote some other letter, lost to us now, where he complained about the food or wanted to know why God had left him in this circumstance and felt sorry for himself. Maybe he knew the emptiness that comes in not laughing for months. If he did, he didn't stay there. Because now we have this witness of joy. "I will continue to rejoice." Where does that joy come from?

Paul rejoices, because he knows that God will deliver him. If I understand him here, he is not stating that he will find a deliverance from the court. He's not even stating that he knows heaven awaits and deliverance comes in its ultimate fashion. Paul's confidence is that, regardless of how Caesar's court may rule, God will be pleased with Paul's witness.[6] Paul quotes Job, who declares, "I know that I shall be vindicated."[7] Paul is trusting that God will declare, "Well done, good and faithful servant."

What is the basis of Paul's confidence? God will deliver Paul by empowering him to exalt Christ. Paul hopes that he does not bring shame on himself but, rather, by the power of God, is able to muster the courage to remain faithful at his trial. Paul has been able to ensure that the guards know of Paul's trust in Jesus Christ. Paul simply wants to remain faithful to this calling. He teaches us that, in the face of the storm, it's not only what God does for us but what our lives can do for God that can be a source of joy. It humbles Paul to know that, with his act of faithfulness, God might be exalted. Exaltation is a word often associated with worship. But here Paul ties exaltation to his faithful daily choices and with speaking boldly of his trust in Christ. The whole of one's life provides the context to exalt God. To think of life as a drama of exaltation to the living God gives us some insight into Paul's spirit of joy, even in the face of hardship.

Paul doesn't speak of happiness that comes from pleasant circumstances but of joy that is born from knowing you are living life the way God intends you to live it, and it glorifies God. This is why Paul rejoices, or as Dr. Bob would say, he is of good cheer.

Tharseo is the Greek word that is translated "I am of good cheer." As I mentioned before, it is found in John 16:33, but it describes Paul. And this is the reason why: *tharseo* is also translated "I have courage." To be of good cheer or to be courageous; the same word has both meanings. An

6. Hooker, "Letter to the Philippians," 490.
7. Hooker, "Letter to the Philippians," 490.

interpreter may be drawn to choose one meaning over the other (in English, it's unavoidable), but the real power of *tharseo* is the recognition that good cheer is often what courage looks like. Or to say it more clearly, to live a life of good cheer or of joy will require courage. The joy that Paul describes does not result from life circumstances falling in pleasant places, but, rather, his joy is a courageous act, sometimes even a defiant act of faith in the face of suffering.

I saw this courageous joy in Stormy. Stormy was a woman who was a little crazy. You never knew what Stormy was going to say or what she was going to do. She was always laughing. She was often playing little pranks. As she often said, "All we need to have a party is to find a day that ends with the letter *y*."

She sang in the church choir, and as the choir processed into worship each week, she would come down the center aisle like she was running for office. She would talk to children, greet visitors, and hug friends. The fact that the congregation was singing a hymn of praise to God was just a backdrop to Stormy's delight in everyone around her. To tell the truth, it bothered me a little bit. I thought she was a little shallow. That was until I learned her story.

Stormy had more than enough reason to be bitter. She had buried two husbands over the years. Her firstborn, Gary, was killed somewhere in the jungles of Vietnam. If that wasn't enough, macular degeneration struck her and left her vision so impaired, she couldn't read the music for the choir anthem. Most would have dropped out of choir. But Stormy stayed, and when it was time to sing the anthem, if she knew it, she would sing it by heart. If she didn't know it, she simply mouthed, "Watermelon, watermelon, watermelon." She said, "No one can tell I have no idea what the words are."

She had every reason to be bitter. But if you had met Stormy, you would have found a woman of good cheer. You couldn't help but smile when you saw her. She gave you the impression that she spent the whole day just waiting for you to walk into the room. Her piety was simple but strong. When she prayed, she didn't pray, "O Eternal Creator"; she prayed, "Hey, Fella, I need you today." Even in times of need, her joyful spirit was remarkably consistent. Her joy was courageous, an act of defiance against the powers that would diminish her. She has been through the storm and yet there was a courageous joy that I can't explain, except to say I saw the fingerprints of God in her life. One of her favorite hymns was:

No storm can shake my inmost calm
While to that Rock I'm clinging.
Since Christ is Lord of heav'n and earth,
How can I keep from singing?[8]

That one she sang by heart.

When Paul says, I will continue to rejoice, I trust him, because I know Stormy, and she lived the same way. In her life, Christ was exalted, and not just in the choir loft but in the choices she made every day.

Philippians 1:21–26

[21]For to me, living is Christ and dying is gain. [22]If I am to live in the flesh, that means fruitful labor for me; and I do not know which I prefer. [23]I am hard pressed between the two: my desire is to depart and be with Christ, for that is far better; [24]but to remain in the flesh is more necessary for you. [25]Since I am convinced of this, I know that I will remain and continue with all of you for your progress and joy in faith, [26]so that I may share abundantly in your boasting in Christ Jesus when I come to you again.

No Choice at All

In verse 21, it seems like everything changes. "Dying is gain." "I do not know what I prefer, to die and be with Christ or to stay here with you." Has Paul's joy abandoned him? Did he muster a brave face for a while, but now the realities of the situation crash down on him? That would be understandable. Folks who face difficult circumstances know how hard it is to stay positive all the time. There are low moments and challenging times. It sounds like Paul is unsure if he wants to continue. Maybe it's time to throw in the towel. "I am hard pressed between the two: my desire is to depart and be with Christ, for that is far better; but to remain in the flesh is more necessary for you" (Phil 1:23–24).

Really? I would prefer to catch the train to glory, but I'll stick around because you need me. In these verses, Paul sounds both depressed and arrogant. I think Paul sounds arrogant, in part, because he was arrogant, at least in comparison to how we wish to speak to one another in our day.

8. Lowry, "How Can I Keep."

I offer no defense for that. But arrogance alone does not capture what is taking place here.

Paul seems all over the map:

I rejoice.

I don't know if I want to live.

But on second thought, I'm going to stick around, because you need me.

What is this?

This bold apostle who can seem larger than life on the one hand, or disconnected from real life on the other hand, is sensing all of this at the same time.

Paul's future is not something he will get to decide. Yet he talks as if he will choose his future. It is more nuanced than Paul simply declaring that he is in control of the circumstances. Prison brings clarity to that which is always true: death awaits, and we do not control it. But Paul speaks of his death as something he can choose; it is the preferred choice. Should he make that choice? There are many reasons Paul might prefer death. One student of the text observes, death can be a "release from the troubles and pain of one often imprisoned and severely abused mentally and physically."[9] We have all known those for whom death comes not as a harsh intruder but as a gift of peace, as a welcomed sleep that recues the weary. Perhaps this was true for Paul as well. But then Paul rejects that this is something he must decide. Paul weighs his decision and determines that it is, in the final analysis, not his decision. There is something more necessary than anything he might wish. Paul is first of all a servant (Phil 1:1) of the Lord, and this remains Paul's identity. As Christ's servant, Paul is called to serve Christ through his relationship with the church. For Paul, the calling of God says less about the called one and more about the caller. The character of God, as a God who calls, has been an element of the biblical witness from the beginning. God is constantly calling. From the first moment of creation, when God whispered, "Let there be light" (Gen 1:1), God has been calling the creation to live to God's glory. The call of God continues with, "Go to a land that I will show you" (Gen 12:1). The call continues with, "You shall have no other gods before me" (Exod 20:3). And with, "Whom shall I send, and who will go for us?" (Isa 6:8). And also, "Come and follow me" (Mark 1:17). Paul is just a part of the long story of a calling God, and responding to this call is not something he sees as optional—which door do I choose—no, it is necessary.

9. Craddock, *Philippians*, 29.

Biblical theologian Morna Hooker says that Paul's attitude is reflected in the words of the Methodist covenant service: "Put me to what you will, rank me with whom you will; put me to doing, put me to suffering; let me be employed for you or laid aside for you, exalted for you or brought low for you; let me be full, let me be empty; let me have all things, let me have nothing."[10]

Paul has been laid aside for God, but he sees even this as an opportunity for God to be exalted. As long as Christ is exalted, Paul will not be ashamed; he will continue to rejoice.

But we might ask, is this really good news? Paul appears to be little more than a tool. Paul would respond by pointing again to the exaltation of Christ. God will use Paul's life or his death, it makes no difference, for Paul is more than happy just to be useful for the redemptive purposes of God.

I wish that I could understand this in a different way. But sometimes being faithful is just something we choose, simply because we know we have been created for the purpose to which we now are faithful. Like a parent who is awakened in the night by a child with a fever, we don't debate if we are going to get out of bed. This is not a moment where personal bliss really matters. You are walking the squeaky floors at 4:00 a.m., because your child is too sick to sleep. It's your calling. Even as you struggle to keep your eyes open, there is a sweet kind of peace, a peace that results from knowing you are doing what is yours to do. I don't think anyone would claim this deep act of love makes them happy, but joy might be the right word to identify this midnight act of parenting. As Paul would say, it's not really something we choose but, rather, something we recognize is simply necessary.

The Long Story of the Gospel

Paul recognizes his imprisonment not as a stand-alone moment in his life but, rather, as one more moment in the long story of the gospel. God's work of redeeming the world can happen without any of us. Grace is the only way to explain that God chooses to include all of us in this gospel work. In the long march of redemption, our days are just a few, but they are our days, and they matter.

In 2004, I moved to Kansas City, which for many, but clearly not all, is serious University of Kansas basketball country. My friend Brant gave me a couple tickets to a University of Kansas basketball game. He said, "Take your son, and be sure you get there in time for the movie." My son went to see the

10. Hooker, "Letter to the Philippians," 492.

game; I went to be with my son. We arrived in time for the movie. It was on the big box that hung from the arena ceiling. Music was playing so loudly, it could puree your spleen. In a few moments, they show the history of KU basketball. James Naismith is there. He invented basketball in Springfield, Massachusetts, and shortly thereafter became the first basketball coach at KU. Fogg Allen is in the video. After all, the old arena is called Allen Fieldhouse. Wilt Chamberlain makes his expected hook shot. You see Danny Manning as a player in the 1988 national championship. And that night, the video concluded with Mario's miracle, the shot that sent the 2008 championship game into overtime. It's all there. The point is clear. You may think you are there for a single game in December, but this moment is more than that. This is a living tradition. This game is only a small piece in a long story, and unless you see there is something bigger going on than just a Tuesday night basketball game with Emporia State, you don't understand what this moment is about.

In similar fashion, Paul says this moment is not defined by prison or struggle or the circumstances of my life: this is a gospel moment. We are all part of the long story that is bigger than we are.

In February of 1968, Echol Cole and Robert Walker died suddenly and tragically as they performed their jobs as sanitation workers in Memphis, Tennessee. Their deaths were met with little reaction by those in power in Memphis. Soon, thousands of public works employees were marching in the streets in protest. It went on for weeks. On April 3, Rev. Dr. Martin Luther King Jr. flew to Memphis to assist in strategy and to offer encouragement to those who were striking.

The evening of April 3, King stood before a weary but energized crowd who had braved a thunderstorm to hear him. In what turned out to be less than twenty-four hours before he was assassinated, he told the crowd, "Like anybody, I would like to live a long life. Longevity has its place. But I'm not concerned about that now. I just want to do God's will. And He's allowed me to go up to the mountain. And I've looked over. And I've seen the promised land. I may not get there with you. But I want you to know tonight, that we, as a people, will get to the promised land."[11]

King is often correctly seen as embodying the prophetic tradition of the faith, standing with the likes of Amos, Isaiah, Jeremiah, and others. But here he echoes Paul: "I just want to do God's will."

I'll admit, I don't often have the kind of strength that Paul and King demonstrate. If I am honest, I don't always want what God wants. I live with

11. King, "I See the Promised Land," 286.

a fragmented heart, often wanting conflicting things at the same time. But I do, at least, want to want what God wants. Paul sounds almost invincible here, and I don't know many folks who are like that. But I have known a few.

Jackie was a young, energetic, beautiful woman who heard words from her doctor that changed her life: "You have MS." For the next forty years, she, with grace and courage, battled the disease that eroded her control over her own body. But it did not diminish her spirit. For her last eight or nine years, she was confined to a scooter. Even then, each Sunday morning during the 11:00 a.m. service, she engaged in a paradoxical battle of weakness and strength. With a body that minimally cooperated and a spirit that would not give up, she would, in full view of the gathered congregation, swing herself on obstinate legs from her scooter into her chair in our choir loft. There, as if she had come to show the rest of us what angels looked like, she would sing praise to God. And she would instruct the rest of us in how to engage whatever battle we might be facing with courage.

For everyone, death will have the last moment in this world. But death is not satisfied with just one moment. No, through fear and anxiety, death tries to steal moments ahead of schedule. Death tries to control hours and days and maybe years before our last moment. Jackie forbade death to have control over any moment other than her last. Until the end, she was vibrant and alive and beautiful, and she was not afraid. From that choir loft, imprisoned in her own way, she was a reminder that we are part of something much bigger than the circumstances of our lives, and someday all of God's children will get to the promised land.

Don't let me make this sound easy. You know it's not. If you have been paying attention to the world at all, you know joy is never easy. Happiness can come. Good circumstances have their season. But joy is rooted in a faithfulness to God—a faithfulness secured by a confidence in God's faithfulness to us.

When times are hard, maintaining trust that this faithfulness, both our faithfulness and God's faithfulness, will lead us to the promised day of Jesus Christ, can be challenging. I have already referred to the powerful prophecy that Dr. King uttered just hours before his assassination in Memphis over fifty years ago. I don't know his inner heart, but I trust that he trusted that promised day would come. As he faced the daily ungodliness expressed against himself and people of color across the nation, it is inspiring that he maintained such hope. That night in Memphis, he told us one reason he could maintain his hope. Before he concluded his sermon in which he carried a nation on his back from the dark nights of Memphis up to Mount Nebo to peer into the promised land of racial justice, he first spoke of the man who introduced him that evening. King stepped to the pulpit, and his first words that night were these: "As I listened to Ralph Abernathy in his eloquent and generous introduction and then thought about myself, I wondered who he was talking about. It's always good to have your closest friend and associate say something good about you. And Ralph is the best friend that I have in the world."[12]

Jesus shows up most clearly in our relationships. It is in our relationships that we find strength and courage. To trust our lives to the promised day takes every bit of holy imagination we can muster, and even then, living towards a life of justice, hope, and compassion can seem too good to be true. So God puts people in our lives who come to us as friends or prophets, as teachers or even singers with diseased bodies but spirits with the strength of steel. God puts those people in our lives, and they give us hints of hope, glimpses of grace, and indications that God's new day is coming. Paul was just such a person for the Philippians, and they apparently were the same for him. Paul has confidence in his deliverance, for the Spirit will be his source of help. But in this same breath, Paul says his deliverance will come because the Philippians—who may have been his best friends in this world—are praying for him. This is why his speaks with such confidence that the day will come when "I may share abundantly in your boasting in Christ Jesus when I come to you again."

I imagine Paul reads over these words one last time to make sure they are right and to make sure they are honest. The apostle reflects on the exhilaration of living life defined by what is necessary. It is a life that will require courage. But, by the grace of God, it can be a life of courageous joy. I know it's true; I've seen lives of courageous joy. And I have heard them sing:

> No storm can shake my inmost calm
> While to that Rock I'm clinging.
> Since Christ is Lord of heav'n and earth,
> How can I keep from singing?

When bodies fail, when dreams are dashed, when the struggle for a better self or a better world leave us exhausted, in the mystery of grace, we can continue to rejoice. Thanks be to God, some days are like that.

---

12. King, "I See the Promised Land," 279.

CHAPTER 4

Seeing the Good

I'M A PREACHER'S KID. I grew up going to church every week, without fail. There were seasons in my life when I protested this infringement on my freedom. I had much better things to do. I was five or six years of age, and I let my mother know I had no desire to go to church. She told me she understood completely, as she felt the same way at times. She then told me to put on my church shoes and get into the car. I was going to church, and my not wanting to go really had no bearing on the matter. You can see I suffered through an oppressive childhood.

I soon stopped my protests, as my mother wasn't going to change her mind. But something else happened as well. I started to feel drawn to worship; I even looked forward to it. Worship may begin as an experience, but soon enough it becomes a practice. It wasn't the preaching that drew me in, not at first. It was the hymns. I loved "Be Thou My Vision" and "Abide with Me." "Be Still My Soul," "The Church's One Foundation," and "Come, Thou Fount of Every Blessing" were some of my favorite hymns. Even now, my hope is renewed when we sing:

> Love divine, all loves excelling, joy of heav'n, to earth come down,
> Fix in us thy humble dwelling, all thy faithful mercies crown.
> Jesus, thou art all compassion, pure, unbounded love thou art;
> Visit us with thy salvation; enter ev'ry trembling heart.[1]

When we can talk about faith, our faith grows. Saying out loud what we believe is one of the important ways to strengthen our faith. But when

---

1. Wesley, "Love Divine."

we sing our faith, it's easier to trust the holy promises on which we base our lives. When times are challenging, we need songs of faith to carry us through. In my own life, I've experienced the power of reciting "The Lord is my shepherd," but there is a different experience altogether in singing "For all the saints who from their labors rest." Music has an honesty that speaks the same language as the soul. The melodies carry memories. I love to sing that great funeral hymn "Abide with Me," and almost every time I do, I am reminded of the hot August South Carolina afternoon, when we gathered in a small whiteboard church to give thanks to God for the life of my grandmother. When we sing one of those hymns with personal history, it's easier to trust that God is in the room.

Paul knew the power of the hymns of faith. When he approaches the most important part of the Philippian letter, Paul turns his readers to a hymn. There is no way to be certain, but were I to provide a little midrash on this passage, I would imagine it was a favorite hymn. I imagine it is not only a hymn they all knew but a hymn that Paul had sung with them. These letters were written to be read aloud in worship, but when they reached this part of the letter, rather than reading it, I imagine they all stood and began to sing:

> though he was in the form of God,
> did not regard equality with God
> as something to be exploited,
> but emptied himself.

But before he invites them to sing, Paul turns our focus to a life that is worthy of the gospel.

Philippians 1:27–30

27Only, live your life in a manner worthy of the gospel of Christ, so that, whether I come and see you or am absent and hear about you, I will know that you are standing firm in one spirit, striving side by side with one mind for the faith of the gospel, 28and are in no way intimidated by your opponents. For them this is evidence of their destruction, but of your salvation. And this is God's doing. 29For he has graciously granted you the privilege not only of believing in Christ, but of suffering for him as well—30since you are having the same struggle that you saw I had and now hear that I still have.

Before We Sing

"Only," Paul says. Just this one thing. It is time for Paul and the Philippians to have a family meeting to talk about the issue of the day. Paul is turning to the meat of his sermon now: "Only, live your life in a manner worthy of the gospel of Christ." This is a bold exhortation and may be one that comes to us unwelcomed. Paul's message is not "you do you," but rather the apostle asserts that the gospel calls us to cultivate our best life, a Christ-shaped life. What does such a worthy life look like?

The Greek word translated to "live your life" is a word that Paul uses only here: *politeuomai*.[2] However, to live, conduct oneself, lead one's life is the third definition of *politeuomai*. The first definition is have one's citizenship or home. *Politeuomai* invites us to think of the gospel as a new home for followers of Christ. To be at home describes less a place we live but, rather, a manner of living. Paul is drawing a distinction: the rights and responsibilities of our lives are not ultimately defined by citizenship in the Roman Empire (and, for many, a lack of citizenship in the empire), but, rather, the responsibilities of our lives are defined by the gospel. *Politeuomai* is also a word that does not describe my home, but our home. Morna Hooker notes, "Paul has probably chosen this particular verb because he thinks of Christian behavior not simply as something undertaken by individuals, but as the expression of the life of the whole community. His meaning is, 'Let your life as a community be worthy of the gospel of Christ.'"[3]

We have heard this before: Christ does not come into our hearts or our heads but into our relationships. The Christian life is a communal life and can't be lived alone. If we were to simplify this point, we would remind ourselves that to follow Christ is to live a life of love. But love can only exist when there is someone else to love. Just as Jesus announced that the kingdom of God has drawn near and then immediately created a community by calling disciples, so, too, Paul indicates a life worthy of the gospel is a life that is shared with others. But be clear, what makes a group of people a community of faith is not a set of doctrines to which everyone agrees, as important as doctrine is. The church is not defined even by a collection of mission activities, although they, too, are important. The church is first a network of relationships. Gospel is essentially ecclesiological—communal.

2. The verbal form of this word is in 1:27. The noun is used in 3:20. These are the only uses of the word in Paul's letters.

3. Hooker, "Letter to the Philippians," 496.

So, citizenship is a helpful metaphor, as the gospel calls us to be mindful that we belong to one another. Paul encourages us to let our life as a community be worthy of the gospel.

This insistence that the life of faith is essentially life shared with others provides a prophetic word to our culture, because individualism is celebrated, perhaps even worshipped, in contemporary America. In some significant ways, the means of practicing community have evolved over the past generation. It leaves us feeling less like citizens of a shared gospel or all parts of one body, as Paul says elsewhere, and more like a collection of individuals.

Popular cultural voices repeatedly tell us that the most significant virtues are not those that bind us to one another but those that enable us to stand independent and on our own. John Stuart Mill was an influential British philosopher of the nineteenth Ccntury. In 1859, he penned a book, *On Liberty*, where he made a case for individual freedom. Mill believed that people should be free to do whatever they want. No one should impose beliefs on another about how life should be lived. There is no ultimate good to be served with one's life other than to live in obedience to one's own needs and desires. Mill argued that the only limitation to personal freedom should be a prohibition on harming your neighbor. You can do anything you wish, just don't hit people. Even if choices create self-harm, well, that's the price we pay for liberty. Mill says, "Over [oneself], over [one's] own body and mind, the individual is sovereign."[4] For Mill, freedom exists when one's choices are unencumbered.

This is the way we experience freedom in our lives. When we have the capacity to make our own decisions, make our own choices, without external obligation or pressure, then we are free. Over my life, I am sovereign. Or to put it more simply, I own myself.

Building on Mill's philosophy, novelist and philosopher Ayn Rand offers a twentieth-century expression of such individualism. She contends that to focus on one's own life is the ultimate virtue. To define one's life in relation to another is oppressive. The free and moral person must live by his or her own standards and therefore "live as [one] pleases, as [one] chooses and as [one] believes."[5] Rand argues that selfishness is a virtue, for it is the person who is guided by self-interest who exerts the will to build his or her own life and not demonstrate dependence on another. To be guided by a form of altruism or care for the neighbor requires self-denial. Yet, for one

4. Sandel, *Justice*, 49.

5. Burns, *Goddess of the Market*, 42.

to be truly moral, Rand argues, one must care for one's own life (who else will?). The self must be the "beneficiary of [one's] own moral actions."[6] In short, obligation to the neighbor is oppressive.

While many would find Rand's attack on altruism somewhat juvenile, we do live in a time when the life of the individual is highly valued and the relationship to the neighbor is increasingly uncertain. Sometimes this individualism is clothed in spiritual metaphor. One of the favorite hymns of the last century is entitled "In the Garden." The chorus lilts,

> And he walks with me, and he talks with me,
> And he tells me I am his own,
> And the joy we share as we tarry there,
> None other has ever known.[7]

I've often wondered, how does the singer know no one else experiences this singular joy while walking and talking in the garden? And why would that be a good thing? We are left to wonder if perhaps the best thing about this garden is that there is no one else there.

Barbara Brown Taylor shares her spiritual experience. She writes:

> I know plenty of people who find God most reliably in books, in buildings, and even in other people. I have found God in all of these places too, but the most reliable meeting place for me has always been creation . . . . To lie with my back flat on the fragrant ground is to receive a transfusion of the same power that makes the green blade rise . . . . Where other people see acreage, timber, soil, and river frontage, I see God's body . . . . When a cricket speaks to me, I talk back. Like everything else on earth, I am an embodied soul, who leaps to life when I recognize my kin.[8]

I love that. I haven't spoken to crickets, but I have camped under the Quetico stars more times than I can count,[9] and I know the spiritual experience of which she speaks. The fingerprint of God can be witnessed in the vastness of the night sky, the haunting notes of a loon's song, or the brightening of the morning sky at sunrise. In similar fashion, like Taylor affirms, God can be met in books, as we search for the words to describe life in an honest fashion. This is all good. But it is also incomplete.

6. Rand, "Why Selfishness," 82.

7. Miles, "In the Garden."

8. Taylor, *Leaving Church*, 79.

9. Quetico is a national park in Canada. I join friends each summer for a few days of canoeing and camping in these remote waters.

James Davison Hunter, sociologist and professor of religion at the University of Virginia, has written about the erosion of communal obligation in contemporary culture. He says, "Community is no longer 'natural' under the conditions of late modernity, and so it will require an intentionality that is unfamiliar and perhaps uncomfortable to most Christians and most churches."[10]

This diminished sense of communal responsibility has been a topic of study for decades. In 1985, Robert Bellah wrote *Habits of the Heart*, which documented an increased individualism in American culture. Bellah was followed by Robert Putnam in *Bowling Alone*, published in 2000, in which Putnam documented the decline of social groups in America—fewer bowling leagues and more bowling alone. More recently, in *The Vanishing Neighbor*, Marc Dunkelman points to how the ways we practice community have undergone a significant transformation, leaving us less skilled in engaging folks who are different from ourselves and thereby further diminishing a sense of responsibility to the neighbor.

In pursuit of individual freedom, we have missed an essential human reality. As the Good Book says, it is not good to be alone. Mill claimed that the only way to be free is to be able to make choices without restrictions. But the only way for choices to be free from obligations to others is to be free of relationships that place expectations on us. A life lived without obligations to another can be lived only in isolation. You can't be a spouse, a parent, or a friend and have your choices unrestrained. You can't love or be loved and have your choices unencumbered. Ultimately, the freedom that Mill, Rand, and others describe is only understood as a freedom from each other. Such understanding of freedom is an immature understanding of freedom; they have confused being free with simply being alone.

David Brooks offers this reflection: "Our society suffers from a crisis of connection, a crisis of solidarity. We live in a culture of hyper-individualism. There is always a tension between self and society, between the individual and the group. Over the past sixty years we have swung too far toward the self. The only way out is to rebalance, to build a culture that steers people toward relation, community, and commitment—the things we most deeply yearn for, yet undermine with our hyper-individualistic way of life."[11]

10. Hunter, *To Change the World*, 227.

11. Brooks, *Second Mountain*, xvii.

No one is claiming that community is ignored. Rather, healthy community, meaningful community, is sometimes viewed not as the intention or goal of human living, but as a by-product that results from an individual life well lived. However, if real community is reduced to a hoped-for consequence for the individual, it is not likely to emerge. For relationships to be healthy, they require intentionality.

In the movie *Cast Away*, Chuck Noland, played by Tom Hanks, is stranded on an island after his plane crashes into the ocean. He's all alone with the stuff of the island and debris from the plane crash that washes up on shore. Included in the debris is a soccer ball, which anyone who has seen the movie remembers. Noland draws a face on the soccer ball and names him Wilson. It is an expression of the human need for community. That need is deep in us and it is holy. But there was more. At one point, Noland attempts to escape the island on a raft he has constructed. During the journey, Wilson is lost from the raft. Noland engages in an unsuccessful attempt to rescue Wilson, and when he fails he cries, "I'm sorry, Wilson. I'm sorry."[12] This moment gives expression to something Paul knows in his marrow. We are not human and certainly not Christian by ourselves. So the nature of our relationships matters. We don't want to let one another down. Not simply because healthy relationships can enrich our lives, but even more so because faithful relationships bear witness to the love of God alive in the world.

It is here that Paul states most clearly that the Philippians are facing their own struggles. They have opponents (Phil 1:28). They also are suffering for Christ, sharing in the same struggle that Paul has (Phil 1:29–30). It's hard to be certain just who these opponents are, and it is unclear as to the particular nature of their suffering. What is not in question is the focus Paul has in the midst of this opposition: the way the Philippians treat each other is of utmost importance. When their love for one another increases (Phil 1:9), that is how they live a life worthy of the gospel (Phil 1:27). Paul says this is of ultimate importance, but he doesn't say it is easy.

How we treat one another is at the core of our faith, and it is hard because the nature of Christian relationships stands in contrast to so much that our culture teaches. And Paul knows, when we come to the difficult stuff, it's time to sing.

12. Broyles, *Cast Away*.

Philippians 2:1-11

[1]If then there is any encouragement in Christ, any consolation from love, any sharing in the Spirit, any compassion and sympathy, [2]make my joy complete: be of the same mind, having the same love, being in full accord and of one mind. [3]Do nothing from selfish ambition or conceit, but in humility regard others as better than yourselves. [4]Let each of you look not to your own interests, but to the interests of others. [5]Let the same mind be in you that was in Christ Jesus,

> [6]who, though he was in the form of God,
> did not regard equality with God
> as something to be exploited,
> [7]but emptied himself,
> taking the form of a slave,
> being born in human likeness.
> And being found in human form,
> [8]he humbled himself
> and became obedient to the point of death—
> even death on a cross.
> [9]Therefore God also highly exalted him
> and gave him the name
> that is above every name,
> [10]so that at the name of Jesus
> every knee should bend,
> in heaven and on earth and under the earth,
> [11]and every tongue should confess
> that Jesus Christ is Lord,
> to the glory of God the Father.

Remember Who You Are

Not only does the Philippian congregation face opponents outside the church (Phil 1:28), but also division within the Philippian congregation is an issue (Phil 4:2). The church is struggling to live in full accord and of one mind (Phil 2:2). The gravity of the discord is debated by scholars, with some suggesting potential schism within the Philippian community as the reason Paul wrote the letter to begin with. Paul writes to encourage unity. But Paul is always concerned about unity. Paul's concern is seen in his repetition: "Be of the same mind . . . being in full accord and of one mind" (Phil 2:2). Internal divisions are always more serious than the external threats. External harassment can create unity. However, the unity of the church must be one that results not from a common enemy but from fidelity to one another. As Fred Craddock has written, "If they cease to act and simply react, then it is no longer the gospel but the culture which gives the church its identity."[13]

Paul's appeal to unity leads him to encourage the church to live in a Christ-shaped pattern. To find our home in this gospel requires that the church live in a Christ-minded fashion. He says, "Let the same mind be in you that was in Christ Jesus." This important sentence is missing a verb. The sentence literally reads: "Let the same mind be in you that ___ in Christ Jesus." For us to make sense of this, English requires us to supply a verb. But which one? The most common choice is "to be": "Let the same mind be in you that is/was in Christ Jesus." Translated this way, Jesus is the example of what Paul calls the Philippians to exhibit among themselves. It's a high calling. Paul points to the mindset of Jesus and instructs, go and do likewise.

Others suggest our condition has been changed by Christ. To use a favorite phrase of Paul's, we are already in Christ. To reflect this change already realized in us, the verse is translated, "Let the same mind be in you that you have in Christ Jesus." Translated this way, Paul reminds the church what Christ has already done for them and exhorts them to live out their new identity. They already have the mind of Christ, but, clearly, they are not thinking with it.

In the movie *The Lion King*, the young lion Simba is the son of Mufasa, the king of the jungle. Mufasa dies, leaving Simba as the heir apparent. Simba is lost in his grief and unable to fulfill the responsibilities this new life casts upon him. In the midst of his despair, the crazy baboon Rafiki tells Simba that Mufasa is actually alive and promises Simba, "I will show him to you!" Rafiki leads Simba to a pool of water where he might gaze in. Simba peers into the still waters and dejectedly says, "It's just my reflection." Rafiki says, "Look harder and you will see Mufasa, your father, lives in you." And then, like the baptism moment from the Gospel of Mark, Mufasa's voice comes from the clouds, "Simba, remember who you are."[14]

In similar fashion, Paul is reminding the church who we are. Christ lives in you, "so let the same mind be in you that you have in Christ Jesus"— remember the truth of who you are.

13. Craddock, *Philippians*, 33.
14. Mecchi et al., *Lion King*.

But Don't Overthink This

Three times in these verses Paul speaks of the mind. "Be of the same mind" (Phil 2:2), "of one mind" (Phil 2:2), "let the same mind be in you that was in Christ Jesus" (Phil 2:5). On the face of it, Paul sounds a bit crazy here. Even in families, people don't have the same mind. People don't think alike. Students of the text recognize that the Greek word *phroneo*, here translated as mind, is better translated as mindset, attitude, or orientation. Thurston and Ryan say "Paul is asking that they be 'minded' or 'disposed' in a certain way, literally 'think the same.'"[15] Think the same? Be careful here. The church has never been the church by people thinking alike.

Actually, over the history of the church, when the church has defined herself by her thoughts, by her doctrine, it has often resulted in division or even schism. Do you baptize believers, or can you baptize infants? Can women preach? Is the Lord's table open to everyone, or do we limit who comes to the table of grace? Is the LGBTQ community welcome or excluded? Church historians remind us that, at times, folks not only stopped worshipping with one another over questions like these, but, in some instances, people lost their lives.

If your definition of church is that we are all going to think the same things, then you are on the road to a smaller and smaller church. If being the church means we have to think the same things, we are doomed. For much of the church's history, we have, intentionally or not, implied that following Jesus is primarily an intellectual exercise: to be faithful is to get our doctrine right. Doctrine is important. Christians need shared language to describe the realities of life in the world, particularly as that life is seen through the eyes of faith. But that shared language or doctrine serves a larger purpose. Discipleship is not simply a matter of getting our doctrine right; discipleship is a matter of getting our relationships right. Our doctrine lives in service of right relationships.

Therefore, to have the same mindset as Christ is not the same as thinking the same things. (Do we really know what Christ thought?) Rather, to have the mindset of Christ is to live in the world the way Christ lived in the world. Paul describes this mindset for them: "Do nothing from selfish ambition or conceit, but in humility regard others as better than yourselves. Let each of you look not to your own interests, but to the interests of others" (Phil 2:3–4).

15. Thurston and Ryan, *Philippians and Philemon,* 73.

The mindset and orientation of Christ is a spirit of humility. Humility is the governing message of the hymn they sing.

> though he was in the form of God,
> did not regard equality with God
> as something to be exploited,
> [7]but emptied himself,
> taking the form of a slave,
> being born in human likeness.
> And being found in human form,
> [8]he humbled himself
> and became obedient to the point of death—
> even death on a cross.

This is a hymn of humility. Humility is not an idea; it's a practice. Humility is not a thought; it's an attitude. Humility is a way of engaging those around you. Here at the center of this letter, Paul lifts up humility as a central Christian practice or attitude.

I have misunderstood humility most of my life. For the longest time, I thought humility was refusing to think too highly of oneself. No boasting, no calling attention to yourself. No one wants to be around a braggart. One demonstrates a humble spirit by keeping in the shadows, directing the conversation away from yourself—"enough about me, tell me about you!"

I failed to notice the irony of this train of thought. How can humility be obtained if I am thinking about myself all the time, even if it is to make sure I'm taking a low profile? This is not the definition of humility that Paul provides. Using an old hymn of the faith, Paul describes the humility of Christ. The Christ hymn speaks of Christ's incarnation, suffering, and death as an act of humility. But Christ did not choose the incarnation because he thought less of himself. Paul doesn't understand Jesus to be some "aw shucks, it's just me" kind of Lord. No, that is not how Christ demonstrates humility.

Humility demonstrated by Christ is not the practice of considering yourself in some "less than" fashion. Christ does not call us to think less of ourselves. Actually, humility is not a way of thinking about ourselves at all. Humility is never a virtue we obtain head-on. Humility is the by-product that results from considering those around us in an honorable fashion. When we see others as valuable, when we see the beauty and the worth of our neighbor, humility is the natural result.

One night in 1973, my dad said, "I want you to meet Johnny when he gets here." "Johnny who?" I asked. "Johnny Oates," he replied. At the time, Oates was the catcher for the Atlanta Braves. "What's he coming here for?" "He's coming to stay with us until the end of the season." "Sure, dad, I bet he is." I was thirteen years old. When you are thirteen years old, having a major-league ballplayer live in your basement makes the second coming of Christ seem anti-climactic. I wasn't falling for it. But sure enough, about midnight, a little sports car pulled into the driveway. Johnny Oates got out of his car. He had no catcher's mitt, no uniform, no cleats. He wore absolutely nothing to let my neighbors know that a major-league ballplayer was in my driveway. But he did have a small suitcase. He had come to live with us for the final eighteen home games of the season.

We sat at the kitchen table and ate a midnight piece of pie. He talked about life on the road, about being teammates with Hank Aaron, and about catching the knuckleballer—Phil Niekro. It was a magical night. But then my dad turned into my dad again. He said, "John, you know Tom is quite a ballplayer. Just last Tuesday, he and Joe Davis turned a double play during the church league softball game." "Dad," I said, "This is Johnny Oates. He is not going to be impressed with church league softball. He's a major-league ballplayer. Just stop talking." (I was thirteen, so, of course, my parents could embarrass me by simply being in the room.) The irony, that could not have been lost on my dad, is that had anyone else been at that kitchen table that night, I would have been more than happy to talk them through the details of that double play. But not this night. Why? I was humbled. I was humbled not because of how I saw myself; I was humbled because I was looking to the guy at my kitchen table with admiration. He was important. He was a major leaguer, and one who took the time to share a few stories with me at midnight. I was humbled, because I viewed him with respect.

Humility is not a condition we achieve head-on. Humility is the result of seeing the good, the valuable, even the beautiful in others. Christ came, because he saw and still sees the value, the worth, and the beauty in the creation God has made, and that includes us. As people of faith, we are to look for the good not just in major league ballplayers but in ordinary folks, including ourselves.

When my kids were in middle school, I got them a telescope for Christmas. I was so excited. It turns out, I was the only one excited about this gift. Sometimes on a clear night, I look through it, since my kids have no need of it. I'm not very educated about the night sky, but you don't need to know much to be filled with wonder. There are so many stars.

In this ever-expanding universe, astrophysicists can only estimate just how many stars there are. Even the number of galaxies remains uncertain. Some estimate that there are between one hundred and two hundred billion galaxies. The closest galaxy to us is the Andromeda Galaxy, and it is 2.3 million light-years away. A light-year is the distance light can travel in a year. Light moves so fast that, were it to work this way, light could circle the earth seven and a half times in one second.[16] So, in a year, it can travel a long way.[17] The most distant galaxies are 13.5 billion light-years away. Some of these stars that we see actually died millions of years ago, but the light is just reaching us now. The smallest galaxies include about one hundred billion stars. Larger galaxies might include a trillion to maybe ten trillion stars. Astrophysicists now estimate there may be as many as one septillion stars; that's a one with twenty-four zeros.[18] Of course, the actual number of stars, God only knows. But it's enough to inspire a spirit of humility in anyone.

If that is not mind-boggling enough, astrophysicist Neil deGrasse Tyson says, "In the beginning, nearly fourteen billion years ago, all the space and . . . matter and . . . energy of the known universe was contained in a volume less than one-trillionth the size of the period that ends this sentence."[19] As the psalmist has written,

> When I look at your heavens,
>   the work of your fingers,
>   the moon and the stars that you have established;
>   what are human beings that you are mindful of them? (Ps 8:3–4)

But God is more than mindful. The God who fashioned one septillion stars and billions of galaxies, the God who created the heavens and the earth, found the one small blue dot in the universe that is our home, and that God chose to take on human form and even to suffer death. Paul tells us the reason Christ humbled himself is because this incomprehensible God loves with a love that cannot bear to be away from you. This is the mindset of Christ: a holy love that calls you by name and cannot bear to be away from you. It is this holy love that is witnessed as the humility of

16. McClure, "How Far."

17. Traveling at 186,000 miles per second, light travels 5.88 trillion miles in a year.

18. These numbers are all estimates, and estimates can vary widely. I have taken these numbers from Howell, "How Many Stars," para 17.

19. Tyson, Astrophysics, 17.

Christ. He is humbled, not because he thinks less of himself, but because Christ sees the beauty, the worth, the value in the creation. Christ is humble because of what he sees in you and in all, and Christ loves what he sees.

We live in a culture that excels in identifying what's broken, particularly in others. We can see the flaw in the argument, the chink in the armor, the weakness in character. That which is ugly or broken or even evil is not difficult to see, because it's always there. This is a beautiful world, but it is also broken, and that brokenness is everywhere and in everyone. As Paul says elsewhere, all fall short. That's the truth; but it's not the whole truth. There is a constant temptation to let ourselves be defined by the worst in us and to let others be defined by the worst in them. But it is faithful to look for the good in one another. That is the mind of Christ. Christ came, lived, died, and was raised, because there is a holy love that sees the good, the beautiful, the value in the whole creation that God so loves. The spirit of humility lives not by denying what is broken in us and others but by recognizing that the broken creature remains beloved by the creator. Christ does not ignore that the world in which he chose to dwell is a sinful mess; it's just that our sin does not ultimately define us. No one is defined by the worst in them but by the best in God. The humble heart sees the world as it is, but it also imagines the world as the power of God's love will make it. In an imperfect world, it takes courage to choose humility and to look for the good. Yet to do so not only creates the power to hold us together in unity, it is also the soil in which the fruit of joy blooms. It is a joy so genuine that at times the only way to express it is song.

"Love divine, all loves excelling, joy of heav'n, to earth come down."

CHAPTER 5

For Example

"It was the best of times, it was the worst of times, it was the age of wisdom, it was the age of foolishness, it was the epoch of belief, it was the epoch of incredulity, it was the season of Light, it was the season of Darkness, it was the spring of hope, it was the winter of despair . . ."[1]

My high school English teacher claimed that Dickens's opening sentence of *A Tale of Two Cities* was the best first sentence of any novel in the English language. My friend Tyler insists that if novels translated into English can be included, then it must be Tolstoy's Anna Karenina: "Happy families are all alike: every unhappy family is unhappy in its own way."[2]

I may have done Dickens a disservice by quoting only about half of his opening sentence, but, even if included in total, my money is on John Irving's novel *A Prayer for Owen Meany*. The opening sentence reads, "I am doomed to remember a boy with a wrecked voice—not because of his voice, or because he was the smallest person I ever knew, or even because he was the instrument of my mother's death, but because he is the reason I believe in God; I am a Christian because of Owen Meany."[3] That's a great sentence!

I'm not sure what a wrecked voice sounds like. In my mind, I hear a strange mix of Dick Vitale and Archie Bunker's wife, Edith. Characters in the novel hate the sound of Owen's voice. They find it grating. One character swears his voice is so piercing, it could bring dead mice back to life. But Owen's best friend Johnny has a different take. He says, "I have apprenticed

1. Dickens, *Tale of Two Cities*, 584.

2. Tolstoy, *Anna Karenina*, 1.

3. Irving, *Prayer for Owen Meany*, 3.

myself to his voice. His cartoon voice has made an even stronger impression on me than has my grandmother's imperious wisdom."[4]

"I have apprenticed myself to his voice." Apprenticing is not as common a practice as it once was. However, when it comes to living a Christ-minded life, we all could benefit from a mentor or two.

Philippians 2:12–18

[12]Therefore, my beloved, just as you have always obeyed me, not only in my presence, but much more now in my absence, work out your own salvation with fear and trembling; [13]for it is God who is at work in you, enabling you both to will and to work for his good pleasure.

[14]Do all things without murmuring and arguing, [15]so that you may be blameless and innocent, children of God without blemish in the midst of a crooked and perverse generation, in which you shine like stars in the world. [16]It is by your holding fast to the word of life that I can boast on the day of Christ that I did not run in vain or labor in vain. [17]But even if I am being poured out as a libation over the sacrifice and the offering of your faith, I am glad and rejoice with all of you—[18]and in the same way you also must be glad and rejoice with me.

We Have Work to Do

After the Philippian congregation concludes the hymn sing (Phil 2:5–11), Paul returns to the business of living a life worthy. He describes salvation as something that requires work. Of course, to work out your salvation is not the same as working for your salvation. Paul would have none of that. Salvation is always God's work. The humbling choice of being born in human likeness, about which Paul just sang, is the means by which salvation enters the world. God's saving work is not limited to the realms of glory but takes place in this world. Christ takes on human form, because our lives in this world matter to God. Salvation is not simply about getting us into heaven but about getting some of heaven into us. And that takes work. Paul says we work out our salvation with fear and trembling. This is not a threat. It's not "work out your salvation, or else!" Fear and trembling is our posture in the

4. Irving, *Prayer for Owen Meany,* 20.

presence of the holy, because there is nothing more important in our lives than living or working out the saving grace that has claimed us all.

I stood in the broad median of a busy, four-lane boulevard. I had come from Charleston, South Carolina, to propose to my girlfriend, who was attending school in Richmond, Virginia. I took an overnight train and arrived before most of the city was awake. It was my girlfriend's birthday, and my arrival was a surprise. (It occurred to me only after I boarded the train that she might have other plans for her birthday.) I called her from a payphone (it was 1985). I invited her to breakfast. We went to Aunt Sarah's, a spot we had frequented the year before, when both of us lived in Richmond. We ate omelets and fruit. After breakfast, we walked down the median of the main drag in town. My plan was to propose that evening at The Tobacco Company. The Tobacco Company is a mid-nineteenth-century tobacco warehouse converted into a restaurant featuring entrées I could not afford. My plan was to propose just before they brought out dessert— Butter Cake for Two. It is a lovely setting to propose marriage. I am sure it would have been lovely for us as well. However, the entire time the train rocked through the Carolinas, I was nervously trying to think of just the right words to propose. And then I spent all of breakfast reaching in my pocket every three seconds to ensure the ring was still there. It was clear to me, given my level of anxiety, I would never last to a 7:30 p.m. reservation, which was still eleven hours away. So, with morning traffic whizzing by, car horns honking here and there, in fear and trembling, I asked if she would spend her life with me. Fear and trembling, not because I was worried she might say no. Like most couples who reach this point, we had talked about marriage on numerous occasions. The fact that I would propose was no mystery; the only questions were when and how. To expect her to be free for her birthday was completely foolish, I admit, but I didn't expect her to say no to marriage. I asked in fear and trembling, because I found a love I wanted in my life, and I knew her answer was of great importance—a source of joy to this day.

Paul says, work out your salvation in fear and trembling, not because you are afraid, but because there is nothing more important in our lives than living or working out the saving grace that has claimed us. This is an invitation or, better said, a calling to trust your salvation. Trust your salvation like you trust gravity; let it influence the choices you make in every moment, in every relationship. It is no wonder Paul speaks of God's work of salvation creating work for us. That work, as Paul understands it, is the hard task of living in a Christ-minded fashion with one another. We do so by "holding fast to the word of life" (Phil 2:16), or perhaps more simply said, apprenticing ourselves to his voice. Paul's testimony is that this work is not something we ever do on our own. No, God is at work in us. The good work that God began in us (Phil 1:6) is a work that continues as we work out our salvation.

Starlight

Paul exhorts the church to treat one another without murmuring or arguing, being blameless and innocent—so much so that we shine like stars. To shine like stars is a pretty lofty description. I love the congregations that I have served, but I don't know that I have ever thought we were the brightest light around. This is one of many places where we might wonder if Paul's metaphors become too optimistic. Paul appears to have forgotten that the folks you meet in church are just like the folks you meet elsewhere. People of faith are flawed and shortsighted. We get grumpy and, more times than we would like to admit, have come down on the wrong side of important social matters. Most communities of faith might just as often resemble the dim light of a flickering candle rather than the brilliant light of a shining star. And that's not simply true of the churches whose failures appear in your newsfeed, but all too often it's the church family you know now, if you know one. When Paul describes the Philippians, or anyone at all really, as "children of God without blemish" who "shine like stars" amidst a "crooked and perverse generation," what do we do with these inspiring but seemingly unrealistic words?

I grew up with a basketball goal in the driveway. I enjoyed shooting baskets, but as a kid of moderate height and less than moderate talent, I was never going to play on a team. Even in neighborhood pick-up games, I was usually chosen after my next-door neighbor, and Brenda was two years younger than I. However, when we gathered to play not in my driveway but down the street at Stuart's house, I played better. I could even dunk the ball at Stuart's house. Stuart had a basketball goal that you could crank down from ten feet to six feet. That fit my game.

For Paul, working out our salvation is not about fitting Christian life to our game. He is not naïve. He knows that our faith journey is one of fits and starts, of struggles, stumbles, and sometimes failures. But Paul refuses to lower the goal, because he trusts that we are not in this journey alone. God is at work in us. That is our hope. The fact that we are loved and claimed by God can influence how we live each day. If we trust that we belong to God, it influences our choices for the better.

In Sue Monk Kidd's book, *The Secret Life of Bees*, Lily finds herself living with sisters, all named after the warmer months. August is the matriarch, and May is the one most in need. Lily, a fourteen-year-old runaway, is welcomed into the home of these wonderful women. The exterior of the house is painted in an impossible-to-miss pink. One day Lily asks August, "How come if your favorite color is blue, you painted your house so pink?"

> "That was May's doing. She was with me the day I went to the paint store to pick out the color. I had a nice tan color in mind, but May latched on to this sample called Caribbean Pink. She said it made her feel like dancing a Spanish flamenco. I thought, Well, this is the tackiest color I've ever seen, . . . but if it can lift May's heart like that, I guess she ought to live inside it."
>
> "All this time I just figured you liked pink," I said.
>
> She laughed again. "You know, some things don't matter that much, Lily. Like the color of a house. How big is that in the overall scheme of life? But lifting a person's heart—now, *that* matters. The whole problem with people is—"
>
> "They don't know what matters and what doesn't," [Lily] said.
>
> "I was gonna say, the problem is they *know* what matters, but they don't *choose* it. You know how hard that is, Lily? I love May, but it was still so hard to choose Caribbean Pink. The hardest thing on earth is choosing what matters."[5]

Choosing what matters is not simply an intellectual decision. Choosing what matters is not like choosing between rocky road or mint chocolate chip. It's not the same as finally deciding to name your daughter Michaela rather than Stephanie, or even choosing where you will go to college. Choosing what matters is a daily practice. Choosing what matters is rooted in character. It must be chosen over and over again. Some days, working out our salvation requires big choices, even significant sacrifice. But salvation is worked out more often through the ritual of routine kindness, mindful attentiveness, and practiced generosity. God is at work in you through all of that.

5. Kidd, *Secret Life of Bees*, 146–47.

For Example

Neighbors—A Very Good Place to Start

Working out our salvation is not something that happens in you but in us. Your own salvation (Phil 2:12) and your faith (Phil 2:17) are second person plural. This salvation work is something the faithful do together. It's a matter of repairing relationships, setting things right, and trusting that God is at work among us.

As we noted in the last chapter, our current cultural context raises particular challenges to communal life. Many of us are surrounded by people on a daily basis, but that is not the same as being connected or in community. The practice of our human connection is changing. It is common to have friends in the virtual world, while knowing those who live in our building or on our street is less common than a generation ago. There is much that is powerful and meaningful in the ability to connect through the ever-changing platforms of social media. At the same time, it has become evident that there is a shadow side to this means of creating community. The curated online presence is sometimes wearying, in that it is a bit too perfect or too clever—or perfectly mundane. But the greater concern is that we now have a dramatically increased capacity to connect with folks who are largely like us in life circumstance and worldview. With clicks, selective news feeds, and hidden algorithms that ensure our worldview is repeatedly reaffirmed, it has become possible to remove from our daily encounters people we might find peculiar or demanding. Becoming surrounded by sameness or something close to it creates a spiritual challenge for those working out their salvation, for salvation is not limited to those like us.

Johnny Wheelwright, Owen Meany's best friend, said, "I suddenly realized what small towns are. They are places where you grow up with the peculiar—you live next to the strange and the unlikely for so long that everything and everyone become commonplace."[6]

Communities that include the strange and the unlikely, as well as those of a differing worldview, teach a set of virtues that, these days, requires discipline and intentionality to learn. When we live with the strange and the unlikely, we learn something of patience and acceptance, but, perhaps even more than that, we learn to trust the good work that God is doing in ordinary folks.

Marc Dunkelman observes that the structures for creating community have evolved in recent America, and, among other things, this

6. Irving, *Prayer for Owen Meany*, 73.

67

evolution contributes to a polarization of society. Reflecting on what Dunkelman calls the township or village community, Dunkelman observes that community was previously structured in three groups or rings, to use his terminology. There was an inner ring that consisted of people you knew intimately—think family and close friends. There was an outer ring that was constituted by people with whom you connected, but usually there was a single circumstance or issue that brought you into contact. These were old friends from elementary school, whom you haven't seen since but who showed up on your Instagram feed; or the barista at your coffee shop; or someone who shared your passion for birdwatching. You were friendly but didn't know what was going on in their lives. Thirdly, there were the middle rings. These were folks who were not intimates, but whom you encountered with a degree of frequency. It's the guy from work with whom you caught lunch on occasion, or even the server, if you eat there enough to order the usual.[7] What is significant and unusual about these middle ring folks is that there is a reason you are not best friends: you aren't that much alike. However, life has put you in contact enough that you appreciate or at least tolerate the differences. With a little patience, you get along.

Dunkelman notes that community was structured with these three rings for most of American history, but that structure has shifted by a reduction of engagement with the middle ring relationships. Most of our social energy is invested in the inner ring and the outer ring. We connect with the outer ring mostly through technology, as online we are able to engage with folks who share our interests or worldview. Indeed, social media is set up to reinforce whatever interest we deem to be important.

Does this matter? Dunkelman argues that it does. When most Americans spent at least a portion of every week engaging in middle ring relationships (Rotary clubs, running clubs, Junior Leagues, PTAs), we rubbed elbows with people who saw things a bit differently than we do. It was Johnny Wheelwright's description of the small town mentioned above: "You live next to the strange and the unlikely for so long that everything and everyone become commonplace." Today, we can spend so much time, in person and online, with folks who by and large see life with the same perspective that we do, it makes it more difficult to recognize the reasonableness or even the humanity of those who see things differently. Building on research by Robert Putnam, Dunkelman claims that when we don't have regular encounters with the peculiar of the world, with people of other social circumstances,

7. Dunkelman, *Vanishing Neighbor*, 96–97.

other political views, other worldviews, what is lost is "our fuller confidence in the goodwill of the average stranger."[8] When I build a network of folks who act and talk and think like I do, I assume that all reasonable people are like me. So if you are not like me, I have to wonder, what's wrong with you? This diminished connection with folks not like me provides room for a meanness, a dismissiveness, an ease in dehumanizing others in our culture. It's easier to assume the worst about others if our patterns of creating community make it easy to lose confidence in the goodwill of the stranger. Consequently, we are not just lonely; we are increasingly afraid.

The point here is not to suggest there were some good old days to which we need to return. Not at all. That would reflect a naïveté about our past, which had troubles enough of its own. No, what is important is to be attentive to the particular conditions in which we work out our salvation during these days. A life defined by the gospel is known only in community. This communal nature of gospel living faces particular challenges in our time but also has particular gifts to offer to a culture that is polarized.

Rev. Fred Rogers, who almost never went by Rev. Rogers, died in 2003. In recent years, a documentary and a movie have been produced about his life and ministry. I used to think he was rather childlike, but that was before I began to learn what maturity actually looks like. Mr. Rogers believed that we could be and should be neighbors. Neighbor was no accidental word. Mr. Rogers reached back into Scripture to find a verse he probably learned at Vacation Bible School: "Love your neighbor as yourself." He leaned on that verse to guide him in complicated and confusing times. For many, he seemed to shine like a star in a dark and conflicted time. This simple but powerful man seemed to rejoice in all whom he met. Many experienced his teaching as a glimpse of salvation, and I can only imagine how much work it was.

To live with one another as neighbors is a good vision for the church. For the first twenty-five years of my ministry, my own denomination was divided over the place the LGBTQ community would have in the church. All the best theological, biblical, and pastoral energy of a generation was poured into this debate. We have settled that issue now, at least for my denominational family, and I am very grateful. But along the way, something happened to us that few of us saw coming. We divided into teams. We learned who was on which side of the issue. We formed friendships with those who thought like we did. We began to circulate in our separate theological silos. We grew increasingly confused and bewildered as we read

8. Dunkelman, *Vanishing Neighbor*, 135.

the same words of Scripture as those on the other side but often heard a different word. We all recited the teaching of our tradition but found divergent guidance. It's probably not too much to say we began to see those on the other side as crazy. Just as importantly, we felt connected to those who saw the world the way we did. The issue determined who our friends were. But then something happened. The church turned her gaze toward a different complex social issue: life in the Middle East. When the national General Assembly met to discuss and vote on certain matters related to the Middle East, it was as if the Holy Spirit slipped into each team's theological locker rooms and mixed up all the jerseys. Regarding the Middle East, we found ourselves agreeing with folks with whom we had had little agreement for over twenty years. Folks we had known to be on our side all of a sudden were lining up behind the microphone on the other side. When the issue under focus changed, the teams we had recognized and relied upon were suddenly all mixed up.

It made me wonder, in a world that is always divided, what would happen if, in the church, we refused to let the issues determine who our friends are but, rather, let our friendship determine how we navigate the issues? What would happen if the church, in her life, refused "to give up on what the faithful God refuses to give up on."[9] Of course, that might take a miracle. But we should not whittle down that dream to fit our current lifestyle. We should continue to work out our salvation with one another, for the truth is, miracles happen when God is at work in us. And God has not given up on us. Were the church to become known not as a community that thinks alike but as a community that loves each other, even when we don't think alike, we would shine like stars in a world captured by the dark night of loneliness, fear, and division. Living in faithful communion like that is not our game yet, but we should not lower the goal to fit our current game.

Philippians 2:19—3:1

> [19]I hope in the Lord Jesus to send Timothy to you soon, so that I may be cheered by news of you. [20]I have no one like him who will be genuinely concerned for your welfare. [21]All of them are seeking their own interests, not those of Jesus Christ. [22]But Timothy's worth you know, how like a son with a father he has served with me in the work of the gospel. [23]I hope therefore to send him as

9. Ottati, *Reforming Protestantism*, 101.

soon as I see how things go with me; ²⁴and I trust in the Lord that
I will also come soon.

²⁵Still, I think it necessary to send to you Epaphroditus—my
brother and co-worker and fellow soldier, your messenger and
minister to my need; ²⁶for he has been longing for all of you, and
has been distressed because you heard that he was ill. ²⁷He was
indeed so ill that he nearly died. But God had mercy on him, and
not only on him but on me also, so that I would not have one sorrow after another. ²⁸I am the more eager to send him, therefore,
in order that you may rejoice at seeing him again, and that I may
be less anxious. ²⁹Welcome him then in the Lord with all joy, and
honor such people, ³⁰because he came close to death for the work
of Christ, risking his life to make up for those services that you
could not give me.

¹Finally, my brothers and sisters, rejoice in the Lord.

Secondary Examples

Paul moves in a rather clunky fashion, at least by the judgment of some students of the text, from soaring exhortation (shine like stars) to travel plans
(I want to come to you . . . but of course, I'm in jail . . . so, I'll send Timothy
. . . but first your friend Epaphroditus). Given that such logistics are often
included at the end of letters, some have wondered if we are reading a frag-
ment from another letter that has been pasted into this letter. I don't find such
explanations necessary or even helpful for our engagement with the text.

Paul says he hopes sometime soon to come visit the Philippians, which
is clearly a reunion for which they all are longing. However, while they wait,
Paul will send Epaphroditus and then Timothy. Both of these persons were
well known in Philippi. Timothy had served with Paul in Philippi, and as
Paul says, the Philippians know his worth. Epaphroditus had been sent by
them to minister to Paul while Paul was imprisoned. Apparently, while with
Paul, Epaphroditus (a name I am grateful was not popular when my parents
were looking through the baby book of names) became deathly ill. Those
who loved him were concerned for him. So, Epaphroditus would visit first,
then Timothy would come, and finally Paul would visit himself. That covers
the logistics.

But, if I understand the text, there is more going on here. Hooker asserts, Paul is illustrating in a "down to earth level . . . what it means for men
and women to live 'in the Lord' (Phil 2:19, 24, 29) and, therefore, to work

out in their daily lives how to share the attitude of Christ."[10] When you are concerned for others, when you love them, that concern shows up. Maybe that's the clearest thing to say about love. In our lives, love doesn't always say the right thing, it doesn't always do the right thing, but it shows up. Returning to the Philippians to share in fellowship and worship, to break bread together—that's ministry. It's mundane, and it's ordinary, and sometimes we can take it for granted, but it is a way the church lives the love of Christ. When those sent by Paul to Philippi arrive, it will be a joyful homecoming.

But there is a second point here. Paul has just exhorted the church to live a life worthy of the gospel, to do so without complaining, and to shine like stars. He doesn't want the Philippians to assume that such a life is beyond their spiritual capacities. So Paul reminds them of Timothy and Epaphroditus. They are inspiring people.

Just as Paul did when he opened the letter, once again, he introduces those who need no introduction. The Philippians know Epaphroditus and Timothy. They don't need Paul to provide a letter of reference or send a resumé. But Paul is guiding the church in how they should think about these friends. Epaphroditus is not just someone they sent to Paul, to support and minister to Paul, but Paul says he is now Paul's "brother and coworker and fellow soldier, your messenger, and minister to my need" (Phil 2:25). Paul invites the congregation to see Epaphroditus and Timothy as "dependent and secondary examples of the Christian life."[11] For all who live in the Lord (Phil 2:19), Jesus is our primary example. Paul has already had them sing about that. But there is a tendency in the church to think, well, Jesus can live this way, but he can walk on water, too; we are not Jesus. We think that way because it's true: there is significant difference between even the greatest saints and Christ. But there are at times also beautiful similarities between Christ and the followers of Christ. If that were not true, then there would be no reason for Christ to have humbled himself to come to us. Paul would be speaking hollow words when he calls the church to live a Christ-minded life if we can't, at times, at least resemble the life of Christ. Perhaps knowing that the Philippians—and we, too—might be skeptical, Paul provides examples. He points to Epaphroditus and says, "I see Christ in him. So I will also see Christ in you. You can do this!"

Even more so, Paul holds up Timothy as an inspiring follower of Christ. Timothy is Paul's son in the faith. Timothy has "served in the work

10. Hooker, "Letter to the Philippians," 521.

11. Migliore, *Philippians and Philemon*, 107.

of the gospel." Given that Paul describes himself as a servant (Phil 1:1), and that Jesus is described as a servant/slave (Phil 2:7), to say that Timothy has served the gospel is a description of faithfulness and grace.

But perhaps the greatest affirmation Paul gives to Timothy is to insist that Timothy can't come right now. Why? Paul will send Timothy "as soon as I see how things go with me" (Phil 2:23). One scholar interprets, "If Paul's situation gets worse and should even come to his receiving a death sentence, it is Timothy whom Paul wants by his side."[12] The apostle needs a pastor; he needs a friend, because often the clearest way to know that Christ is here is for Christians to be here. For Paul, Timothy is both his son and Christ's servant.

Of course, Paul is not just stating his need for Timothy, but he is once again saying to the Philippians, "I see Christ in Timothy. So if Epaphroditus can reveal Christ, and Timothy can reveal Christ, you, too, can reveal Christ's presence in the world."

I was driving with my wife to an evening fundraiser for the Midwest Innocence Project. I was grumpy, because we were running late. We were running late, because I had gotten stuck at the church in a meeting and arrived home to pick her up leaving no time to spare. During the ride to the downtown hotel dining room I was, once again, short. The whole day had been stressful, and I didn't want to embarrass myself by arriving after everyone had finished their salads. It's not like we could just slip in, for, in this instance, we were to be seated at the head table. My wife said, "We will be fine." She was right. We arrived in time to meet everyone at our table before things got under way.

The Midwest Innocence Project is an organization that endeavors to free those who have been wrongly convicted. An elder in the church was on the board of MIP and invited us to sit with her and her husband; that's the reason we were at the head table. The keynote speaker would be at our table as well. The keynoter that evening was John Grisham, author of about a thousand books. My brother gives me the latest Grisham novel each year for my birthday. They are great vacation reads. All his books are fiction, except one. *Innocent Man* tells the story of Dennis Fritz and Ron Williamson, who were wrongly convicted of murder. I knew I would get to meet John Grisham, but I hadn't expected I would be able to sit next to Mr. Fritz. He spent eleven years imprisoned for a crime he did not commit. If he had been a bit short, I would understand. Mr. Fritz was eventually exonerated.

12. Migliore, *Philippians and Philemon*, 108.

He was going about his life now, but no one could do a thing about the eleven years lost. That's the hard thing about injustice; it can sometimes be addressed, but it is seldom made right. And yet, as we chatted that evening, there was no bitterness in Mr. Fritz. I can only assume there had been bitterness and anger at some point, but there wasn't a trace of it that night. He was comfortable with himself and with others. He laughed quickly and was attentive when listening to others. There was a peace about Dennis Fritz that was unmistakable. He actually seemed joyful.

Had it been just my wife and I sharing dinner at home that night, I am confident I would have taken a good portion of the evening to talk about how stressful my day had been. But sitting next to the innocent man, I gained some perspective.

I'm not suggesting that Mr. Fritz is grounded like this all the time. I imagine he still battles his demons, and that sometimes they get the best of him. He's not Jesus. But at least that night he was what Migliore calls a secondary example of the Christian life. It was an example that inspired me and made me want to be more like what I sensed in him.

Christian faith is embodied in the lives of ordinary saints. We never get it perfect. Every last one of us stumbles. It's hard to string too many days together without doing something that no doubt embarrasses our Lord. But that is just part of our story. The other part is that we are also apprenticing ourselves to Christ's voice. We are apprenticing ourselves to Christ's example. It takes all we have, yet, at the same time, it is God at work in us. So, even in us, that good work that God has started (Phil 1:6), God will continue to bring to completion. The work of salvation will show up. Love always shows up. You have seen God at work in others. Like Paul, I imagine you could develop your own list of those who have been brothers and sisters, coworkers, and holy messengers in your life. Give thanks to God for the fingerprints of the holy that you witness in them; and then let them inspire you to trust that, by grace, God is also striving toward the completion of that good work in you.

CHAPTER 6

Heading Home

I CAN STILL HEAR my mother as she raised the kitchen window to call to me in the back yard. I was, no doubt, roughhousing or perhaps swinging a stick in a careless fashion. She called, "Tom, put that down. You could poke someone's eye out!" This was a frequent reprimand in my childhood. She was so enthusiastic in her parental guidance, you might think that there was an epidemic of one-eyed kids in my neighborhood, but that was not the case. I knew some kids who wore glasses, but I didn't know anyone with an eye patch. Another favorite saying of hers was, "If you don't stop that, I'm going to hang you by your thumbs." Sometimes she threatened to skin me alive. There was no need to call the Department of Child and Family Services. We both knew that she wasn't going to torture me; if the truth be told, she had a hard time simply putting me in time-out. The threats she launched into the back yard were obvious hyperbole. She used strong language, even exaggerated language, because something important was at stake. She didn't want me to injure myself or someone else. Unlike the apostle, I imagine the frequency with which she had to say the same things proved to be troublesome, even exhausting, for her. But to her, not causing injury to others was important, so she pressed on: "Put that down, I told you!"

Three times in Phil 3:2, Paul shouts, "Beware!" Beware of the dogs, the evil workers, and the mutilators! I don't know if Paul was being hyperbolic or not, but I do think it is the only way we can read his words in our day. We take Paul's warning seriously, but also, for several reasons, we take his warning cautiously. One reason we proceed carefully is that none of us is pure. But also, the two thousand years of the history of church has taught us that the use of denigrating language has too often led to the justification of violence. I think my mother and Paul are on the same page. We need to be careful not to hurt one another, particularly not to use our faith as the weapon. That's important.

Paul raises his voice to provide a safeguard for the Christians in Philippi. With repeated exhortations, he tells them this is important. As disciples, we need to remember what is important, but, in doing so, the good news of the gospel can never become bad news for our neighbor. Let us embrace the text with care.

Philippians 3:2–11

To write the same things to you is not troublesome to me, and for you it is a safeguard.

2Beware of the dogs, beware of the evil workers, beware of those who mutilate the flesh! 3For it is we who are the circumcision, who worship in the Spirit of God and boast in Christ Jesus and have no confidence in the flesh—4even though I, too, have reason for confidence in the flesh.

If anyone else has reason to be confident in the flesh, I have more: 5circumcised on the eighth day, a member of the people of Israel, of the tribe of Benjamin, a Hebrew born of Hebrews; as to the law, a Pharisee; 6as to zeal, a persecutor of the church; as to righteousness under the law, blameless.

7Yet whatever gains I had, these I have come to regard as loss because of Christ. 8More than that, I regard everything as loss because of the surpassing value of knowing Christ Jesus my Lord. For his sake I have suffered the loss of all things, and I regard them as rubbish, in order that I may gain Christ 9and be found in him, not having a righteousness of my own that comes from the law, but one that comes through faith in Christ, the righteousness from God based on faith. 10I want to know Christ and the power of his resurrection and the sharing of his sufferings by becoming like him in his death, 11if somehow I may attain the resurrection from the dead.

This Is Garbage

Paul writes, "Beware of the dogs, beware of the evil workers, beware of those who mutilate the flesh!" Dogs. Evil workers. Flesh mutilators. Paul moves from joy to condemnation in a heartbeat.

Paul provides a word of caution as well as a reminder of what is important. He cautions the Philippian church about folks the apostle believes have missed the theological boat. There is some uncertainty regarding the identity of those who find themselves caught in Paul's forensic crosshairs. Some believe Paul was calling out a group of Jewish Christians who were insisting that the grace of Christ is insufficient for salvation. These are sometimes called Judaizers.[1] They insist salvation depends on the faithful observance of particular Jewish practices. As a result, the gentile believers, who do not maintain these practices, remain outside of the true faith. The terms dogs, evil workers, and mutilators are terms that Jews had sometimes used to describe gentiles who remain outside the true faith.[2] Therefore, when Paul uses these same terms to describe Jewish followers of Jesus— those who were drawing the line to declare who is in and who is out—there is a bit of irony, as Paul turns the tables on the Judaizers. The foundation of Paul's experience and theology is that the grace of Christ is sufficient for salvation. Therefore, Paul asserts that the gentile Christians do not need to take on Jewish practices. It is those who find the grace of Christ insufficient and needing to be supplemented by human acts of faithfulness who are standing outside the faith. This ancient theological debate is not as hotly debated in our day. However, Paul's caution remains relevant to us in this fashion: when we start drawing lines to declare who is in and who is out, Jesus will often be found with those on the other side of our line. Limiting both the expansiveness and the effectiveness of God's grace is risky business. Beware!

A second observation from these verses is that these folks, Jews or gentiles, have become confused about what is important. To quote the old saying, they have confused the finger that points to the moon with the moon. They have stumbled over what Paul calls confidence in the flesh. Confidence in the flesh is the opposite of how Paul has described the mind of Christ (Phil 2:5–11), so it cuts to the heart of the matter. One scholar has stated, "Those who mock earthly privileges are usually people who do not

---

1. Thurston and Ryan, *Philippians and Philemon,* 112.
2. Hooker, "Letter to the Philippians," 524.

have them."[3] This is not the case with Paul. He challenges these boastful people to compare resumés. His privileges resulting from birth are significant. His accomplishments are impressive. He can play their game. But then Paul says, all of this he regards as loss because of Christ. Just as Christ did not regard equality with God as something to be exploited, Paul does not regard his reasons for confidence in the flesh as something to be exploited.

Paul says privilege that results from birth and upbringing, as well as practices of faithfulness, have their place, but they are not ultimately important. Paul should know. He was born to the right people, and he never missed worship. He followed the law perfectly. He was passionate about his faith. In matters like these, Paul is willing to stack his personal history against anyone's. He is confident he will win. But winning is the problem. When winning is the focus, dependence on God gets lost. Placing confidence in our own faithfulness tempts us to diminish our dependence on the saving grace of Christ. In this sense, winning is actually losing. All these measures of status and achievement Paul regards as loss, even as garbage. They are not regarded as loss in and of themselves, but, rather, in comparison to knowing Christ as Lord, they are garbage (and that is translating it nicely). In these verses, Paul tells us how sharing the mind of Christ has changed what he regards as most important. Like disciples who, at the drop of a hat, drop their nets, the apostle drops his privilege and accomplishments and depends solely on the saving grace of God.

The first time I watched a soccer game, it was played by boys and girls about five years old. My son was among them. Every Saturday morning, he and other kindergarteners ran or sometimes skipped out onto a field with a soccer ball. They didn't really play positions; it was more like herd soccer. They just amoeba around, oozing first one way, then another. Now and then, someone kicks the ball, and it rolls across the chalk line into the goal, and the entire team jumps up and down. They do throw their little fists into the air. Sometimes kids from the opposing team cheer as well. After all, the point is to get the ball in the net; why be picky about which net?

There are few low-scoring games with a team of five-year-olds; there is frequent scoring. This makes it hard for parents to keep up with the score. We were often asking one another, "Is it 5–4, or are we tied?" Parents worry about that. And parents worry about skill development. Is my kid getting better? Parents also worry about the rules: "Who is that big kid? He looks

---

3. Hooker, "Letter to the Philippians," 526.

like he could be in second grade!" Parents worry that the coach is playing the Johnson kid more than my kid. But, mostly, parents worry about the score.

One Saturday, the last whistle blew, and the evil empire had won in the neighborhood of twenty to two. I listened as my friend Cheryl knelt down to comfort her son, Joey. "Son, I'm so proud of you. You played hard, and you ran fast. I saw you kick the ball several times. You can't always win, even when you do your best." I was impressed. I thought it was good parenting in a disappointing moment. That is, until Cheryl said, "I'm sorry you lost." Joey looked to his mother bewildered and said, "We lost?"

Every Saturday, there were two games going on. There was the game the kids were playing, and there was the game the parents were watching. The kids were playing a far better game. From the sideline, it can be really difficult to remember what the game is for.

Paul is speaking to what faith and faithfulness are for. He has not turned his back on the importance of religious practices. After all, Paul has said we must work out our salvation in fear and trembling. Faithfulness matters, but it doesn't save us. We are saved by what God has done in Christ. Faithfulness is the joyous response to being claimed, loved, and included in the family of God. For Paul, this is what matters most. It's not the status he has gained by birth or discipline. It's not experiences that set him apart. Those things matter, but they do not matter ultimately. Paul is illustrating again what the spirit of humility, demonstrated in Christ, looks like in his own life. All these conditions and circumstances that give him confidence in the flesh are set aside, as it were, because Paul has a new identity, a new purpose, and a new understanding of what matters in the world.

What matters most is to know Christ. And the Christ Paul knows is the Christ who did not profess confidence in the flesh but, rather, humbled himself. We are saved by the faith we see in Christ. There is a lively discussion among scholars of how to translate the Greek text. Some translate it faith *in* Christ (Phil 3:9). Yet, it can also be translated faith *of* Christ.[4] This latter translation is consistent with Paul's focus on the saving act of Christ. It is he who saves us. Any faith we might have is a result of the faith that first lived in Christ. If I understand the text, Paul is saying, here is the safeguard, you are not saved by the love that is in your heart; you are saved by the love that is in God's heart. Salvation is God's work.

4. Hooker, "Letter to the Philippians," 528.

But Don't Throw the Garbage Out

So, what about all that garbage (rubbish, Phil 3:8)? Does this mean our practices of faith are irrelevant? No. It's not that binary. We are often tempted to make things more important than they are.

It is a common human failing to confuse things that are important with that which is ultimately important. It matters if you lose a soccer game by double digits, but it doesn't matter the most. At the same time, it is equally problematic to say, "If it's not ultimately important, it's not important at all." For example, worship doesn't save us. But worship is important.

David Brooks talks about the difference between what he calls resumé virtues and eulogy virtues. He says, "The resumé virtues are the ones you list on your resumé, the skills that you bring to the job market and that contribute to external success. The eulogy virtues . . . get talked about at your funeral, the ones that exist at the core of your being—whether you are kind, brave, honest or faithful; what kind of relationships you formed."[5]

Brooks makes the case that eulogy virtues are more important than resumé virtues. True enough, but both are virtues. Being a good father is more important than being a good auto mechanic. But, if you are a mechanic, it's still important that you know how to change out a fuel pump. This conversation about the relationship of grace to religious practices is not a binary conversation for Paul. He does not set before us door number one or door number two and encourage us to choose one. What is at issue is how the salvation that is ours in the faith of Christ relates to the salvation we must work out with fear and trembling. Faith practices do not save us—even when engaged with fear and trembling; but faith struggles to survive, much less thrive, without practices.

Here's what I mean. The practice of praying at mealtime is important. Does it save you? Of course not. Does it make you righteous? Not really. But it reminds you that life is a gift from the gracious hand of God. Table prayers remind you that you are a child of God. Praying reminds you that ordinary things, like eating, happen within the realm of faith and faithfulness. The lordship of Christ affects all of life. When we remember that faith touches every aspect of our lives, not simply at the Lord's table in the sanctuary, but also at our own table in the breakfast room, we are doing more than eating raisin bran for breakfast; we are working out our salvation.

---

5. Brooks, *Road to Character*, xi.

A faith that is not practiced will get lost in abstraction. The life of faith must be grounded in religious practices of various kinds—prayer, worship, generosity, service—all of which form the community of faith. If we do not practice our faith, it diminishes and becomes as nutritious as cotton candy. But we cannot confuse our spiritual practices with the faith itself. Viewing our practices as the same thing as the faith itself reduces the faith of Jesus Christ to, well, garbage.

Ultimately, Paul knows we stand before God as beggars claimed by a holy love that calls us by name and will never let us go. That love is both the gift we have received in Christ and the model we have received from Christ.

Blind Spots

Before we move on, it is appropriate to circle back to whom Paul had in mind when he felt compelled to once again offer this safeguard. Morna Hooker and others interpret them to be folks who were Jewish by birth or conversion and also Christian, who believed more was required to belong to the family of God than the grace of Christ.[6] For Paul, this is a conversation about the grace of God; but for many in the church, through the years, it has been a conversation about Judaism. It has often been an unholy conversation that has led to unholy acts.

Shortly after Easter of 2019, a young man, still a teenager, carried an AR-15 into the synagogue in Poway, California. The shooter is named John Earnest. He is a Presbyterian. That is not just a casual detail. Earnest asserted that he entered the synagogue with an assault rifle because his faith called him to do so. He even pointed to the apostle Paul as a source of inspiration for this act of violence. In fairness, Earnest's pastor and congregation, including his parents, were shocked. They certainly did not interpret the gospel as a justification for violence. In the wake of the horrors of September 11, many Muslim Imams and scholars came forward and publicly said, "This violence is not of Islam." I realized in Eastertide of 2019, it was our turn to do the same. This violence is not Christian.

I imagine, like me, you find religiously inspired violence heartbreakingly misguided. But we should do more than condemn such misguided theological convictions. We should learn what is ours to learn here. As we noted in chapter 2, when we meet someone, anyone, who in our own assessment we deem to be different from ourselves, the universal human

6. Hooker, "Letter to the Philippians," 525.

temptation is to see them as lesser than ourselves. The difference can be almost anything. It can be race or religion. It can be economic status or cultural observance. When in our own spirit we meet one who seems different from ourselves, it is a powerful temptation to see them as lesser, to equate difference with deficiency. To do so is to claim a certain confidence in the flesh, rather than to share the mind of Christ in humility. In short, whenever the good news of Jesus Christ becomes bad news for our neighbor, we can rest assured we have a blind spot somewhere.

John Earnest had a blind spot. Many do. Actually, all of us do at times. And not simply through anti-Semitism. The church has stumbled over a wide variety of prejudices and cruelties. The church has and often continues to belittle women, for example, or folks of other faiths or people of color. The history is undeniable and pervasive, and it's why we engage this text with care. Anytime we have used the gospel as a weapon to injure a neighbor, we can assume Christ is being crucified once again with that neighbor. To bear witness to what you believe is a good thing, but to do so by declaring your neighbor is a dog or evil worker . . . well, put that down, for we have already poked someone's eye out. It was ours.

Philippians 3:12–16

> [12]Not that I have already obtained this or have already reached the goal; but I press on to make it my own, because Christ Jesus has made me his own. [13]Beloved, I do not consider that I have made it my own; but this one thing I do: forgetting what lies behind and straining forward to what lies ahead, [14]I press on toward the goal for the prize of the heavenly call of God in Christ Jesus. [15]Let those of us then who are mature be of the same mind; and if you think differently about anything, this too God will reveal to you. [16]Only let us hold fast to what we have attained.

Press On

Paul has said he wishes to be found in Christ (Phil 3:9) and to know Christ (Phil 3:10). One scholar has said to be found is not a possession but a home in which we belong.[7] Christ as home is a helpful image, but not if we think

7. Migliore, *Philippians and Philemon*, 130.

of going back home. Frederick Buechner says that we all have a home in our memory. Many of us speak of going back home. But more than back there, says Buechner, home is something for which we are constantly longing. He says, "I believe that what we long for most in the home we knew is the peace and charity that, if we were lucky, we first came to experience there, and I believe that it is that same peace and charity we dream of finding once again in the home that the tide of time draws us toward."[8]

Home is ahead of us. Paul clearly understands that being found in Christ launches a journey. He says he has not already reached the goal. The Greek word translated as "reached the goal" is *teleioo* and also means to complete or bring to perfection. Paul is not perfect. We aren't either. But this is not a confession that we make mistakes along the way. It's larger than that. To be perfect or to reach the goal is to finally become the person God intends you to become. Like the hymn says, "Finish then thy new creation, pure and spotless let us be."[9] Paul understands that all of us are to be shaped by the mind of Christ, the life of Christ, the love of Christ, to the point that we are Christlike ourselves. We aren't home yet. But Paul is pressing on, straining forward (Phil 3:12–14). He sounds like an athlete here. He's straining forward in confidence, trusting as he said at Phil 1:6 that the good work God has begun, God will bring to completion. So, tomorrow can be a new day, not just yesterday lived all over again.

But the pursuit of a life of faith is not pure. We are sloppy with it at times. We stumble and experience setbacks. Even when we get it right, we discover we have not arrived, but Christ has raced ahead, and we are still left to follow. The disciple is always in the position of following.

Ben Comen ran cross country for Hannah High School in South Carolina. He wasn't great at it—at least he wasn't fast. But he drew a crowd. When asked why they watched, some said because it was beautiful. Ben not only never won the race; he never beat anyone across the finish line.

Ben had cerebral palsy. It had not diminished his intellect, but it seized the muscles and contorted his body, leaving him to lunge and falter. Simple stones and twigs could present a problem and cause him to fall. Still, Comen ran the just over three-mile race. In almost every race, he fell, and when he fell, he fell hard, because his body couldn't react quickly enough to catch himself. It was not unusual for Ben to cross the finish line bloodied about the elbows and knees. By the time he finished, every other runner

8. Buechner, *Longing for Home*, 3.
9. Wesley, "Love Divine."

had had time to shower and go get a cheeseburger. But they didn't go anywhere. They waited. Not only his teammates but kids from the other teams waited. When he neared the finish line, they all returned to the track and crossed the finish line together. And then they jumped, they clapped, they screamed. Grown men watched, twisting their jaws, trying unsuccessfully to keep the tears off their cheeks.

Rick Reilly of *Sports Illustrated* asked, "Why do they hang around to watch the slowest high school cross-country runner in America?" Reilly's answer is, "Because Ben Comen never quits."[10] It's a good answer. It can be inspiring to see someone with persistence like that. But I also wonder if they watched Ben because they were so much like him or, more likely, they wanted to be like him. Ben said, "I feel like I have been put here to set an example . . . you can either stop trying or you can pick yourself up and keep going. It's just more fun to keep going."[11] People gathered to watch knowing they weren't always good at the things that matter most. They watched him because they know what it is like to live life stumbling and falling. I'm not talking about constrained and unresponsive muscles; I'm talking about fear and selfishness and violence that leave our souls somewhat spastic and held in check. It's the greed and the self-centeredness that leaves our hearts confined and our hopes curbed. It's the blindness we battle when we see someone unlike us and fail to see that Christ is already in them. When they watched him run, he reminded them that you don't have to be particularly good at something to do a particularly good thing. He inspired all who saw him to press on.

The good news is today is a new day and we can press on, straining toward the goal to make it our own, in the sure and certain hope that Christ has made us his own. And one day we will find our way home.

Philippians 3:17–21

17Brothers and sisters, join in imitating me, and observe those who live according to the example you have in us. 18For many live as enemies of the cross of Christ; I have often told you of them, and now I tell you even with tears. 19Their end is destruction; their god is the belly; and their glory is in their shame; their minds are set on earthly things. 20But our citizenship is in heaven, and it is

10. Reilly, *Worth the Wait*, para. 1.
11. Reilly, *Worth the Wait*, para. 7.

from there that we are expecting a Savior, the Lord Jesus Christ. [21]He will transform the body of our humiliation that it may be conformed to the body of his glory, by the power that also enables him to make all things subject to himself.

Transformation

Paul turns the focus away from those who live as enemies of the cross to those who are examples in sharing the mind of Christ by recognizing that the citizenship of the faithful is in heaven, from which we expect a Savior. Paul declares that home is elsewhere. We live here, but we belong there.

Like any good preacher, Paul pays attention to who is in the room, and he piles up vocabulary that would resonate with the Philippians. The word translated citizenship is the Greek word *politeuma*. Paul doesn't use this word anywhere else. Also, Savior is an unusual word for Paul, as it is found nowhere else in his letters. But Paul is taking these political words and placing them in the context of faith. The Philippians would have associated these words with Rome. Some were surely citizens of Rome, where Caesar is the supposed savior. But Paul insists it is not Caesar but Christ who is our Savior. Some may have been proud of their Roman citizenship, while others may have been slaves and therefore held no citizenship at all.[12] Paul promises all of them, you have a home in Christ. Christ is where you belong.

It might be accurate for Christians to think of ourselves as holding dual citizenship, belonging to this world but also belonging to heaven. A better metaphor might be to say we are refugees, caught in a land that is not our home but journeying to the place we all belong. This is what James K. A. Smith affirms when he says, "Your hometown is the place you're made for, not simply the place you've come from."[13]

Paul describes the salvation of Christ as transforming "the body of our humiliation that I may be conformed to the body of his glory" (Phil 3:21). The word body is important in Pauline theology. The Greek word is *soma*. *Soma* is not flesh but, rather, the whole person. *Soma* is not just body but somebody. We don't have *soma*; we are *soma*. When Paul speaks of the transformation of the body, he is not implying our bad hip is renewed or we no longer have a need for eyeglasses. He confesses that that which makes

12. Hooker, "Letter to the Philippians," 535.
13. Smith, *On the Road*, 48.

people who they are is made new. The transformation required is from a body of humiliation to the body of his glory. Like all matters in Christian faith, it is not my body, but our bodies—our *selves*—that are conformed to his body of glory. Paul admits that to live as a disciple is to suffer and even to know humiliation. Suffering is not an aberration that needs to be explained but an expectation that needs to be battled. And Christ has won the battle. We will celebrate that victory in all its glory on God's promised day. We will become who God intends us to be.

Dr. Victor Dzau is a brilliant physician and the president of the National Academy of Medicine. The academy has launched what they call the Grand Challenge in Healthy Longevity.[14] The purpose of this grand challenge is to extend the human life span while keeping bad knees and hearing loss, not to mention weak hearts, from eroding quality of life. They aren't just contemplating adding a few years. The boldest among them are convinced that science can make death optional.

In 2017, there was a fundraiser to benefit Healthy Longevity. It was held in Norman Lear's living room, outside of Los Angeles. Sergey Brin and Larry Page were there. They are the co-founders of Google. Jeff Bezos, the founder of Amazon, was there. Like the rich man who came to Jesus asking "what must I do to inherit eternal life," the room was jammed with powerful folks and Hollywood glitterati, all wanting to learn from the scientists the secrets of healthy longevity. Tuxedoed servers circled the room with delicious finger foods. Goldie Hawn asked about glutathione. It's an antioxidant that protects mitochondria. Some call it the God molecule. Dr. Joon Yun stated that aging is like a code in the human genome. The code can be hacked, he told an enthusiastic crowd. We can end aging. Dr. Aubrey de Grey, the chief science officer of a Silicon Valley research foundation, asserts we can retool our biology and stay in our bodies forever. Dr. de Grey doesn't expect to live long enough to witness this step toward immortality, so he has left instructions to be frozen in liquid nitrogen and thawed when the technology to achieve immortality is available.

I have preached enough Easter sermons that the words eternal life are not foreign to my vocabulary, but I have to say, this quest for immortality sounds like a terrible idea. I'm all for extending the life span a bit, but the idea of making death optional is terrifically foolish. What this project fails to recognize is that addressing our finitude is not our greatest concern.

---

14. Friend, "Silicon Valley's Quest," para 3. The information in this paragraph is gleaned from Friend's article.

Addressing our sin is a far greater concern. Resurrection is not just about eternal life; it is about transformed life. As human beings, we are beautiful but also broken. As communities, we have moments of compassion and fairness and grace, but every community also carries realities of injustice and exclusion. There is a better *soma*, a better self, that is waiting to be breathed to life.

Joe Moll was small and quiet, and yet he is one of the strongest men I have known. He looked fifteen years older than he was, as for a portion of his life he did his best to destroy himself with alcohol. But he dried up. When I met him, he was running Tradition House, a halfway house for men run by the Riverside Presbyterian Church in Jacksonville, Florida. On any given night, there were twenty-four men living in that suburban house, fighting to put their lives back together. Many of them failed. But every day Joe was there teaching, caring, loving these men into a new tomorrow. I asked him what kept him going. He said, "Tom, you have to trust that there is a better man buried down in each one of these men, and it will require a persistent love to bring that better man to life."

Joe did not spend much of his time reading the apostle Paul, but Joe knows the transformation of which Paul speaks. Joe has lived it. The transformation is the fruit of a holy and persistent love that takes the fragile pieces of the lives that we offer and transforms them into a holy self—a *soma* of glory.

I don't know how you think of what Jesus called the kingdom of God or what Paul calls the promised day of Jesus Christ. Maybe you think of the outcasts and the passed-by being seated at the table of grace. Maybe you think of the folks down at the food pantry busy working crossword puzzles because finally everyone has enough to eat. Maybe you imagine the day when our children can "grow up to be neither the destroyers nor the destroyed."[15] Maybe you think of finally being set free from the injuries that enslave us and the burdens that seemingly can't be shaken. The Scriptures are filled with images and metaphors that point us to that promised day, that ultimate home. However you think of it, it's not something that can be described simply as eternal. It is a new self, a new world, that at our best we are straining toward, pressing on. We do so with confidence. There is not anything in our history that suggests it is logical to expect transformation—save the persistent love that was witnessed in the one who embodied that love and has therefore made us his own. All of our stumbling acts of

15. Kingsolver, *Animal Dreams*, 299.

faithfulness come out of and also point to that holy love. That holy love will one day bring to completion not just the dreams we have for the world but the dreams that God has for God's world. Nothing is more important than that. So, even in our spastic and stumbling ways, we press on. In God's good time, we will find our way home.

CHAPTER 7

The Lord Is Near

IN OUR MARRIAGE, IT was curtains. I've known some for whom it was recycling. For another couple, it was the brand of coffee. But for us, it was curtains.

We had been married less than a year and were renting a chopped-up little house devoid of character or warmth. The walls were dark paneling. The floors were old shag carpet and linoleum. Most of the doors of the kitchen cabinets either stuck or wouldn't close completely. But it was home, our first home. I was an associate pastor for a medium-sized church, and she was the head nurse of the oncology unit at a local hospital. After working all day caring for patients, she came home and got to work making our little house a bit more homey. She had saved some money and bought fabric to create some window treatments for the windows in the den. We couldn't afford enough fabric for curtains, so she planned to create some swags. She worked with the fabric for hours, designing several different presentations for how the fabric could decorate and bring color to our drab den. I returned home after being at an evening meeting at the church. She asked me, "Which of these do you like best?" I took in the work she had done and offered my choice. "I think the one on the left; I like how it drapes there." "Oh," she said, "this other one seems a bit more robust to me. Don't you think?" Neither of us remember exactly what happened next, but somehow this simple inquiry about curtains dissolved into quite an argument that lasted the rest of the evening and left both of us feeling injured. The next morning, we ate our breakfast in silence. It didn't end there. This argument about curtains was like the cat with nine lives and for years would resurrect itself into arguments that had nothing to do with curtains.

It was just curtains, but a simple disagreement provided space for deeper division and pain. We don't argue as much as we once did, mostly because I have grown up a bit. I had a lot of growing up to do. When we do, I am grateful that curtains are never mentioned. But for a long time, it was a wound we didn't know how to heal.

Most faith communities can name the times their church family had a disagreement. It's painful. And the pain can last. When disagreements in the church grow so intense that they lead to division, few find it possible to forget.

There was disagreement in the church in Philippi. Some think it was so severe, the disagreement is the reason Paul writes this letter. That's unlikely. There are good reasons to assume the disagreement was actually relatively minor. However, the disagreement wouldn't have to be significant for Paul to speak to it. There never was a time when the apostle took lightly disagreement or division in the church. Even in Philippi, which is a mature community of faith, disagreement in the flock, even if minor, demands the apostle's attention. As I said, I find it more likely that the issue was minor. And yet, even in minor things, Paul says, pay attention. Small disagreements can become large divisions if we allow them to. When the church is fragmenting, it is never our best witness to the Christ who humbled himself.

Philippians 4:2–3

2I urge Euodia and I urge Syntyche to be of the same mind in the Lord. 3Yes, and I ask you also, my loyal companion, help these women, for they have struggled beside me in the work of the gospel, together with Clement and the rest of my co-workers, whose names are in the book of life.

Sing It Again

The Christ hymn that describes what it is to be Christ-minded (Phil 2:5–11) never drifts far from what Paul wants to teach. "Be of the same mind," he encourages again (Phil 4:2). For Paul, theology is never abstract but takes on flesh, and this time he gets specific. Euodia and Syntyche are singled out by the apostle because they are in disagreement about something. What are they arguing about? Who knows? In other letters, when there was disagreement in the church, Paul often provides advice or weighs in on the argument. Paul chastises the Galatians for turning to another gospel (Gal 1:6). With the Corinthians, among many issues, he responds to the report he receives from Chloe's people (1 Cor 1:11). And in the previous chapter, he warns them to beware of the evil workers (Phil 3:2). But whatever the issue is between Euodia and Syntyche, Paul leaves it alone. Elsa Tamez states, "The issue is probably not important from a theological or ethical perspective because Paul does not side with either one of the women."[1]

If the disagreement is not about something significant, we might wonder why Paul has to call these women out in front of the whole church. Why doesn't he just leave it alone? No harm, no foul. There is a reason that Paul can't do that. He knows that disagreements, even over small things—like curtains—can create the space for deeper arguments that result in injury or even schism in communities. So, he reminds Euodia and Syntyche, and the entire Philippian congregation, of the hymn they have already sung: be of the same mind.

Whatever the topic was, it was obviously something important to these women, but the reason Paul cannot keep silent is because he believes their relationship is more important than their disagreement. The church in Paul's day was a lot like the church in our day, and there is no limit to the creativity that the church can muster when it comes to finding something to disagree about. We don't know what they disagreed about, but we do know that these women were leaders in the church. Paul appreciates them as "they have struggled with Paul in the work of the gospel." Their names are written in the book of life (Phil 4:3). The fact that they are recognized as leaders in the church makes their disagreement more significant. When our leaders disagree, the disagreement can spread through the whole church.

So, once again Paul urges them to be of the same mind. Comments on Phil 2:1–5 note that having the same mind is not the same thing as thinking the same thoughts. Euodia and Syntyche are in disagreement, because they don't think the same. It might be assumed that to have the same mind, one of these women has to change her mind, be convinced of the flaws in her perspective, and come to agreement with the other. But that misses the point. They don't actually have to change what they think to have the mind of Christ. No, to have the mind of Christ is to share the orientation of humility that was found in Christ. We are not always going to agree with one another. It is an unreasonable hope that in some great tomorrow, the

---

1. Tamez, *Philippians, Colossians, Philemon*, 103–4.

thoughts of all the people in the world would align and harmony would emerge, because, after all this time, we at last see the world in exactly the same way. It is equally unreasonable to assume that all those who will never see things the way we do will just go away. Paul's vision for the church is a community that learns to stay in relationship, even when we see things differently. The exhortation in this letter is to do what can be done to ensure that disagreements, which inevitably arise in the church, do not devolve into division.

We All Need Some Help

Paul knows that having the same mind is a lofty demand. So Paul pleads for help. He appeals to my loyal companion (Phil 4:3) to help these women. Who is Paul's loyal companion? And why does Paul not mention his name? Regarding the latter question, Elsa Tamez suggests it may be to protect this person. Paul's letters are likely being read by the Roman guards, and for some reason, the loyal companion may be at higher risk of persecution or may be arrested like Paul himself.[2] This is a reminder of the risk that simple confession of faith in Jesus Christ has posed for the faithful at different times and places in the world. As to who exactly this person is, scholars have identified a potential list of candidates longer than my Christmas card list. Was it Silas? Or perhaps Luke? Maybe Timothy or Epaphroditus? Some have suggested it was Lydia. Karl Barth suggests that my loyal companion refers to the whole church.[3] Who Paul's loyal companion is remains unclear, but it is assumed the Philippians knew exactly to whom Paul referred. We can remain in the dark regarding the identify of the loyal companion, but this is the truth: to be our most faithful self is seldom something we can achieve on our own. We all need help along the way. We need others to point out what we fail to see. We need others to help put our thoughts in perspective. We need others to model humility and testify to grace. None of us becomes our best self by ourselves. At the same time, Paul acknowledges that he needs help as well. He loves these women. Paul wants them to reconcile. It is important to him that they stay in relationship. But Paul is limited in the support he can offer from jail. And maybe, even if Paul was in the room with them, he would still need support. It can be hard for leaders to say out loud that they need help, but Paul demonstrates the humility to

2. Tamez, *Philippians, Colossians, Philemon,* 105.
3. Barth, *Epistle to the Philippians,* 120.

admit his limits. So he appeals to his loyal companion for help, because Eudoia and Syntyche need some help, and Paul does, too.

On March 4, 1801, presidential power passed from John Adams to Thomas Jefferson. Jefferson had been Adams's vice president. But Jefferson believed Adams's policies were too sympathetic with monarchy. So, Jefferson ran against Adams in the election of 1800, and Jefferson defeated Adams.

The campaign had been so bitter that these former friends—Jefferson the author of the Declaration of Independence and Adams the voice of independence—ceased speaking to one another. Their estrangement lasted for over a decade.

On January 1, 1812, at the urging of their mutual friend, Dr. Benjamin Rush, Adams broke the silence. He rose above his pain and wrote a letter to Jefferson. This renewed a relationship, and over the next fourteen years, they wrote 158 letters to one another. These once bitter enemies reconciled and corresponded until their death. On his deathbed, Adams's last words were spoken of his friend, "Thomas Jefferson survives." He could not have known that five hours earlier, the very same day, Jefferson, too, had died. It was July 4, 1826, fifty years to the day after together they had signed the Declaration of Independence.[4]

In some ways, Dr. Benjamin Rush is the hero of this story. Without his encouragement—as a loyal companion—these former presidents may never have reconciled. Reconciliation is a bold task for anyone. When there is a disagreement, the issues often seem more important than the relationship. Therefore, we are tempted to determine first what side of the issue we are on. Whom do we believe is right? We want to stand on the side of the right. That is an important decision to make. In no way does having the mind of Christ imply that we somehow stop thinking about or cease to have conviction about issues. But having the mind of Christ does recognize that determining the rightness of a position or choosing the right side of an issue does not complete our work. Believing that we are right on whatever the issue of the day may be very satisfying. And in that satisfaction, we can assume we have done all the gospel requires of us. But Paul insists that there is more work to do, for we are still in relationship with those on the other side of the given issue. We still have to deal with those who do not see things our way. The apostle teaches that it is not enough to be right; we must also be righteous. They sound the same, but righteousness is a

4. McCullough, *John Adams*, 644–46.

word that describes the nature of our relationships. To be righteous is to be in right relationship with God and with neighbor. Perhaps the strongest witness to Christ the church can offer is, when there is disagreement, to work at reconciliation, so that disagreement does not devolve into schism. In my imagination, I believe Paul was asking the loyal companion to come alongside and remind Euodia and Syntyche just how much they meant to the whole church and how much they have meant to one another. Don't be quick to give that up.

In a Flannery O'Connor short story, Mrs. McIntyre inherited a run-down farm somewhere in the rural South, in some yesterday. She has a few African American workers whom she calls by another designation. Also living on the farm is Mr. Guizac, a war refugee from Poland. Mrs. McIntyre calls him the Displaced Person. Mr. Guizac knows his way around a farm, can fix anything, grow anything, and he works like a machine. But he doesn't know anything about American racism. He crosses the line by treating everyone like they belong. Even though Mr. Guizac is the best help she has ever had, Mrs. McIntyre determines she must fire him. She "has no other choice," she says. She knows he has nowhere else to go, but she says, "I don't find myself responsible for all the extra people in the world."[5] It's a tragedy, she admits. But what can she do?

Mrs. McIntyre's priest, Father Flynn, pays her a visit and reminds her that Christ calls us to love our neighbor. He wants her to see Mr. Guizac as her neighbor and one whom faith calls her to love. She says, "Father Flynn! . . . As far as I'm concerned, . . . Christ was just another [displaced person]." Then she says, "I'm going to let that man go."[6]

The way O'Connor writes the story, when Mrs. McIntyre says, "I'm going to let that man go," you can't tell if she means Mr. Guizac or Jesus. But the truth is, it doesn't matter. If she lets either of them go, she lets both of them go.

The church disappoints all of us sometimes. If you haven't experienced that before, give it time, the church will disappoint you. And when that happens, it is very tempting to say, "I'm going to let them go." In that moment, we all need a loyal companion to come along beside us and remind us just how important it is that we hold on to one another.

5. O'Connor, *Complete Stories*, 226.

6. O'Connor, *Complete Stories*, 229.

Perhaps because Paul trusts that Euodia and Syntyche will live in a Christ-minded fashion again and reconcile, he returns to a familiar word: "Rejoice in the Lord. Again, I say rejoice."

Philippians 4:4–7

[4]Rejoice in the Lord always; again I will say, Rejoice. [5]Let your gentleness be known to everyone. The Lord is near. [6]Do not worry about anything, but in everything by prayer and supplication with thanksgiving let your requests be made known to God. [7]And the peace of God, which surpasses all understanding, will guard your hearts and your minds in Christ Jesus.

Near, But Not Here—But Also Here

Paul begins what appears to be a loosely connected train of thoughts. Rejoice. Be gentle with one another. Do not worry about anything. Pray and let God know what you need. The peace of God will guard your hearts.

It's not the smoothest transition from his having just lifted up the disagreement in the church. Yet, as we have seen multiple times by now, the presence of painful circumstances or disappointing realities does not make joy impossible. Paul doesn't simply say "rejoice" but, rather, "rejoice in the Lord." He knows that there are issues in Philippi. He also knows that his prison bars are too strong for him to break. But he trusts that the "sentry of God"[7] will stand watch over him, to ensure no ultimate harm may come to him. Paul is not suffering from denial. Paul simply knows that there is nothing Caesar can do to him that will undo what God has done for him in Christ Jesus, and therefore the peace of God is guarding his heart, his mind, his life. This is the reason that even in the face of suffering and pain, Paul can rejoice.

Can joy be commanded? Not a chance. But the Christian can be attentive to the ways joy can be "awakened, strengthened, and shared."[8] Somewhat mysteriously, that attentiveness may be most easily practiced not when all is well but when we find disappointment in the day. This joy

7. Lowry, *Low-Back, Ladder-Back*, 8.
8. Migliore, *Philippians and Philemon*, 162.

in the Lord is not the same thing as happiness. As Barth described it, joy is a "defiant 'Nevertheless!'"[9]

This defiance is reliable because the Lord is near. There is a mystery in this faithful affirmation. Joy in the Lord is not separated from suffering. The Lord is the One who humbled himself and suffered death on a cross (Phil 2:8). His resurrected lordship does not deny his suffering, but it is all part of a mysterious whole. Therefore, for the disciple there is an element of joy in the Lord that can be understood fully only when we also suffer with and as the Lord did. I cannot fully explain this, but it has been the testimony of many through the ages that suffering, while never celebrated, is not evidence that the Lord has abandoned, or forgotten, or turned aside from God's children. No, rather, it is sometimes in the midst of the hardest times that it becomes clear that the Lord is near.

The first congregation I served was in Charleston, South Carolina. There was a woman in that congregation named Carla. Carla never missed worship. She was always at the early service, and afterwards she made her way to the coffee pot for a cup of coffee and conversation. People were drawn to Carla like waves to the shore. She was always joyful. She laughed easily, even if what was said wasn't really funny. Everyone wanted to talk with Carla, because she was one of those people who just made you feel better. She could lift your spirits. She was a bit of sunshine.

I admired her, but I didn't know her story. Once I learned her story, I was amazed by her. Carla's husband was a sailor. He was not a professional sailor, but it was his passion. He taught their boys to sail, and they knew their way around a boat by the time they were in middle school.

Their son Phillip graduated from college, and he and some buddies took the boat and headed out to sea. Carla said the storm came out of nowhere. It took them days to find the boat. They never did find the boys.

As Carla shared that story with me, I couldn't imagine how this joyful woman I saw every Sunday at coffee hour carried such intense heartbreak. In one of my more stupid moments, I asked, "Carla, you are so happy now, how did you ever get over your grief?" She just smiled and said, "Tom, mothers don't get over that. But I learned something when I was in the valley of the shadow. It took a long time, but I began to see that we all have sadness. Everyone knows the long winter night of the soul. Everyone knows heartbreak. I know what that is like. Every day the sadness is waiting. I don't know if it will come with my coffee and the morning paper, or if it will

9. Barth, *Epistle to the Philippians*, 120.

speak to me in the grocery store, or if it will penetrate my dreams. day I pray, God, don't let the sadness win. Let me push back the s: only in my life, but in the lives of everyone I meet. It's not much "and you may think it's silly, but I think this is my ministry. Ever , try to push back the sadness."

Carla knows what Paul means when he says, "Rejoice in the Lord, for the Lord is near." Joy is not a denial of pain or hardship. This joy is a defiant nevertheless.

To claim the Lord is near is not the same as claiming the Lord is here. Of course, in other places, Paul speaks of being in the Lord, which sounds like Christ is indeed fully present now. This inconsistency or tension actually speaks honestly of our experience with the presence of Christ. On the one hand, the Lord is here now. That is why in the face of hardship and heartbreak, saints like Paul and Carla can push back the sadness and rejoice. Because Christ is here, Paul has reason to be confident that ordinary church folks like Euodia and Syntyche, as well as folks like you and me, can be of the same mind. We gain glimpses of Christ's presence among us in ways that cause us to trust, even in times of distress, that we are not alone. We see the fingerprints of the holy in ordinary time, because the Lord is here.

However, the lordship of Christ or the promised day of Christ (Phil 1:6) is not complete. The good work that God is doing is a work in progress. There is a fullness of Christ's reign when every knee bows and every tongue confesses his lordship (Phil 2:10–11). We live toward that day, but we have yet to see that day. In this sense, the Lord is near but not here. Not yet. And that, too, is a reason for hope. Paul lives his life confident that the good work that God has done will be brought to completion, and the whole of creation is living toward that day. Migliore says, "Even if the word *hope* is not found in Philippians, the reality of hope in Christ . . . suffuses the letter."[10]

At the end of 2016, the *New York Times* noted the most frequently read article over the course of the year was written by Alain de Botton and was entitled "Why You Will Marry the Wrong Person."[11] A surprising title to be the most frequently read article! De Botton says we are all complex human beings who look completely normal only to those who do not know us very well. This creates a challenge when folks are first meeting one another, particularly if that meeting is a date. On a first date, we would all want to put our best foot forward and make a good impression. But de

10. Migliore, *Philippians and Philemon,* 151.
11. De Botton, "Why You Will Marry," para 2.

Botton suggests a more fruitful approach to the first date is not to try to impress one another with how wonderful we are but, rather, to explore a more honest self-reveal. He suggested teeing up a conversation like this: "I'm crazy like this . . . how are you crazy?"[12] If that's how a first date starts, I don't know if the chances are good that it will lead to a second date, but I think I understand why so many people read his article. We know we are a mix of both beauty and brokenness.

The lordship of Christ is not complete in you or me, in the church, or anywhere in the world. We witness the incompleteness of Christ's lordship in the ways that Caesar's power continues to oppress and in the ways that people are divided from one another. But we also see this brokenness in ourselves. Frances Spufford has said, "Wherever the line is drawn between good and evil, between acceptable and unacceptable, between kind and cruel, between clean and dirty, we're always going to be [walking] on both sides of [that line]."[13] It's not an accidental thing. As Spufford says, "It's our active inclination to break stuff, . . . including moods, promises, relationships we care about and our own well-being."[14]

Spufford is providing a definition of what Scripture calls sin, and it's a good definition. Spufford's assertion that it is our active inclination to break things, even the things we care about, is on target. To this reality, Paul offers a word of hope and encouragement, promising the Lord is near. This is a pastoral word; it is also a demanding word. Because the Lord is near, it is incumbent upon people of faith to do the work of faith that is ours to do this day. Because the Lord is near, we seek to live the mind of Christ on this day, until the good work of God comes to completion on the day of Christ.

Frederik Backman's novel *Us against You* narrates life in a small town, where life is defined by ice hockey. Kevin is a teenager and a hockey star. Everyone says he will play professionally. But Kevin has messed up his life. He sexually assaulted a classmate. As is often the case, most folks chose to believe the hockey star rather than the assaulted classmate. But Kevin's friend, who witnessed the attack, musters the courage to tell the truth. As a result, people no longer know how to treat their hockey star. And Kevin doesn't know what to do with this part of his life that he cannot fix. In a moment of shame, Kevin asks his mother, "Do you think it's possible to become a different person?" His mom, carrying the heartbreak of knowing

12. De Botton, "Why You Will Marry," para 2.

13. Spufford, *Unapologetic*, 33.

14. Spufford, *Unapologetic*, 27.

her child abused another, said, "No. But it's possible to become a better person."[15] She's right.

There is much that we cannot repair in our lives and in our communities. There are things that have gone wrong and they can't be made right; they can only be redeemed. Part of the work of redemption is leaning into the possibility that tomorrow can be a new day, not just yesterday lived all over again. It is possible to become a better person. It is possible to become a better church. It is possible to become a better world. We are not home yet. We have not arrived. We, our children, and our children's children's children will still be captured by the "active inclination to break stuff," even things we love. But we can get better. Paul is confident not because he holds great confidence in Euodia or his loyal companion or us, but because he has seen the power of Christ at work in the world and has staked his life to that good work as his North Star.

On September 17, 1987, the country engaged in a bicentennial celebration of the drafting of the United States Constitution. Chief Justice Warren Burger retired from the court so he could preside over this event. That day in Philadelphia, Burger said, "If we remain on course, keeping faith with the vision of the Founders, with freedom under ordered liberty, we will have done our part to see that the great new idea of government by consent—by We the People—remains in place."[16]

Associate Justice Thurgood Marshall offered an alternative interpretation of the event. Marshall became known to many first when he argued Brown v. the Board of Education before the Supreme Court in 1954, the landmark suit that set aside "separate but equal" practices in education. In 1967, Marshall became the first African American to sit on our highest court. Marshall saw the bicentennial celebration of the Constitution through different eyes. Associate Justice Marshall advised that we be wary of what he called the "flag-waving fervor" surrounding the bicentennial. Marshall explained, "The government the Framers devised was defective from the start, requiring several amendments, a civil war, and momentous social transformation" to better realize the promise of a more just society. Credit for the Constitution in its present meaning belonged not to the Framers, Marshall concluded, but "to those who refused to acquiesce in outdated notions of 'liberty,' 'justice,' and 'equality,' and who strived to better them."[17]

---

15. Backman, *Us against You*, 8.

16. Graetz and Greenhouse, *Burger Court*, 1.

17. Graetz and Greenhouse, *Burger Court*, 1–2.

Marshall believed in America, but he could do so only because he knew that America was still becoming. The nation cannot be defined by some yesterday, not even our great ones. I think Marshall was teaching us, if America is to be America, we must be defined by a tomorrow we have yet to see. It is an America toward which we are still living.

I think the same is true for the church. The church is still becoming. The lordship of Jesus Christ is still unfolding. His lordship is near, but it is not here, not fully. We are not home yet. Therefore, the church cannot be defined by our yesterdays, not even our grand ones. The church must be defined by a tomorrow we have yet to see. But we know that tomorrow. It is the day when the promises of the prophets will be fulfilled, and justice will roll down like waters, and all of God's children will be treated as God's children. It is a day when swords will be beaten into plowshares. It is a day when the grumbling noises of children's empty bellies will be replaced with songs of table blessings. It is a day when all that has gone wrong in us and in the world is made right. It is the day of Jesus Christ, when the good work that God has begun in us will be brought to completion.

In the moments when in your own faith you can trust in that day, you will find it easier to rejoice. Even if that joy is an act of defiance against the brokenness of the present day, it is nevertheless a joy in the Lord.

CHAPTER 8

Glory

CLARENCE DARROW BECAME AN internationally known attorney in 1925 when he traveled to a small Tennessee village called Dayton. He was there to defend John Scopes in what became known as the Scopes Monkey Trial. John Scopes was accused of teaching evolution in public schools. Scopes had done just that, and, as a result, he was convicted. But the reporters from across the country were less interesting in the verdict than in how Darrow dismembered the fundamentalist argument of the Presbyterian statesman, William Jennings Bryan, who was the prosecuting attorney.

The year before, in a lesser-known case, Darrow defended two college students named Leopold and Loeb. They were charged with the vicious murder of a fourteen-year-old boy. Nathan Leopold and Richard Loeb perpetrated this cruel and careless murder simply to demonstrate that they were smart enough to get away with it. They weren't and they didn't. Darrow saw the case as an opportunity to argue against the death penalty. His closing argument lasted twelve hours. Here it is (not all of it!):

> Your Honor stands between the future and the past. I know the future is with me, and what I stand for here; not merely for the lives of these two unfortunate lads, but for all boys and all girls; for all of the young, and as far as possible, for all of the old . . . .You may hang these boys . . . . But in doing it you will turn your face toward the past . . . . I am pleading for the future; I am pleading for a time when hatred and cruelty will not control the hearts of [us all].[1]

1. Larson and Marshall, *Essential Words and Writings*, 238–39.

Darrow said, "I am pleading for the future." So was Paul. Deep in the heart of the apostle is the courage to imagine a better world. The calling of the church is to live in the world we know, shaped by the hope we hold in Jesus Christ. Christiaan Beker says it this way, "The vocation of the church is not self-preservation for eternal life but service to the created world in the sure hope of the world's transformation at the time of God's final triumph."[2]

Philippians 4:8

[8]Finally, beloved, whatever is true, whatever is honorable, whatever is just, whatever is pure, whatever is pleasing, whatever is commendable, if there is any excellence and if there is anything worthy of praise, think about these things.

Whatever!

Paul describes a virtuous life by providing a list: whatever is true, honorable, just, pure, pleasing, and commendable. Scholars note that the list of excellent and praiseworthy virtues is not uniquely Christian. Many of these virtues would be found in the culture at large. There is appropriate humility displayed here as Paul looks to the secular culture and finds examples of a virtuous life. Christian faith has always lived in one particular culture or another. Christianity is not an abstract set of beliefs and practices that can be handed unchanged and unchanging from one generation to the next. The Christian is always defined and confined by the particular time and culture in which she lives. Faithfulness, therefore, is the series of moments of sin and grace that are embodied in the lives of people living in particular times and places. There is no such thing as abstract Christian faith. We can't point to Christian life without also pointing to life in Jerusalem or Rome or Kenya or Kansas. Christianity is inescapably particular. At the same time, no culture, not even the culture of the early church, provides a pure Christian witness. To live a life of faith is not to live exactly as they did in Philippi or Philadelphia. Christianity is not about copying another culture but about bearing witness to the lordship of Christ within the culture in which we find ourselves. The lordship of Christ always embraces as well as rejects aspects of every culture. To know what to embrace and what to reject

2. Beker, *Paul the Apostle*, 313.

demands wisdom. That wisdom begins by recognizing that the church does not have a monopoly on God, and the fingerprints of Christ will be found outside the church in whatever is pure, honorable, and just. In some ways, the secular culture may live in more faithful ways than the church. There have been numerous times when the church has had to catch up with the culture in order to be faithful. We should not be surprised that Paul, who describes the Lord as humble, would call the church to be humble regarding the values of our particular culture and to look for the good in and out of the church. Like every Christian, every community falls short of the life that God intends, so looking for the good may not always be easy. We may find it easier to recognize the injustice and the failure of those around us. We may more easily recognize a lack of kindness and pervasiveness of fear around us. But, with wisdom, we might also witness the fingerprints of God in the world each day. It's worth looking for.

Philippians 4:9

9Keep on doing the things that you have learned and received and heard and seen in me, and the God of peace will be with you.

Imitate Me

It's hard to read this verse without rolling our eyes. The apostle says, you guys aren't trying hard enough to be like me. I have preached for over thirty-five years, and never once have I preached a sermon entitled "Be More Like Me, and the God of Peace Will Be With You!" There are many verses in Philippians addressing humility, and it seems Paul has forgotten them all. But to see Paul as simply arrogant misses some important nuance in this verse.

There was an assumption that was common in Paul's age that is much less common in our day. We should read these words in the context of Paul's time. In Paul's day, it was assumed that anyone who wished to develop a virtuous life, anyone who wished to become a mature person, would need some models, some examples. Imitation was a common way to teach virtue.

As we said, Christian faith is not an abstraction but an incarnate reality, always living imperfectly in a given culture. Equally so, Christian faith lives imperfectly in a given person. But Christianity is always embodied. Migliore asserts that when Paul calls the Philippians to imitate Paul, he is calling them to imitate his own imitation of Christ.[3] Therefore, Paul is not holding up himself in an ultimate fashion but, rather, pointing to Christ. Krister Stendahl writes, "We find that there is hardly a thought of Paul's which is not tied up with his mission, with his work. The 'I' in his writings is not 'the Christian' but 'the Apostle to the Gentiles.'"[4] In other words, when Paul calls attention to himself, he is pointing to what Christ has done for Paul and through Paul. It is this working out of salvation that is worthy of imitation.

In as much as Paul is mindful of being a servant of Christ, he is pointing not to his competency or faithfulness as much as he is pointing to the grace he has received and to his calling to live as a servant. As one whose life is good and bad, strong and weak, much and little, it is all defined by the grace of God revealed in Jesus Christ. It seems safe to assume that whatever else the Philippians believed about Paul, they agreed he was God's servant. He preached to them and they trusted him—or trusted what God did through him. As Paul highlights the grace of God in his own life, this moment that otherwise might sound so arrogant is better understood as an expression of gratitude. To imitate Paul is to trust that your own life is defined by the grace of Christ.

My own experience bears witness to the embodied nature of Christian faith. As we have said, Christianity is not simply lived in particular cultures but embodied in communities of people. In my wallet, there is a worn piece of paper on which I have inscribed some names. I've never shown the list of names to anyone, including the folks whose names are written there. But for years, that scrap of paper has traveled with me every day. I don't look at it every day. Actually, very few days do I read over this list of names, but I never fail to do so on the days that I need to. This list of names identifies folks who have taught me something of what it means to be a disciple of Jesus Christ. They have embodied faith, they have practiced hope, and they have shown me what love looks like. Two of them you might know, as they have been my teachers not in person but through their public witness. The rest, you would not know. They have been a part of my life personally. Not one of them is perfect. In most of them, I have witnessed failings or shortcomings. But I have also seen in them grace and humility. Each has demonstrated something of the life of faith that I wish to embody myself. I carry their names with me, because on days when my own faith is fragile, it helps to remember the grace I have seen in each of them.

3. Migliore, *Philippians and Philemon*, 155.
4. Stendahl, *Paul among Jews and Gentiles*, 12.

For clarity, not one of these friends on my list has ever said to me, "Tom, I think you should be more like me." If they did, I doubt they would be on my list. In our context, folks are not likely to offer themselves as models for faith and faithfulness. That's a good thing. But it is therefore wise for us to seek out and pay attention to those who might, in some way, model faithful living. Someday, when your own faith is fragile, you might want to look over a list of names of those who have loved you into faith. To follow Christ is not a small thing. It takes everything we've got. So all of us, at times, need to see Christ alive in someone else. We all need teachers, mentors, models. Choose wisely, and carry their names with you.

Paul is inviting the Philippians to trust that the same grace of God they have seen in him is already at work in them, and that is the source of their peace. Paul doesn't need to give them that peace, they just keep on doing what they have seen in him, keep on doing as they evidently are already doing, and the peace of God will stand sentry watch over their hearts.

Philippians 4:10-14

> [10]I rejoice in the Lord greatly that now at last you have revived your concern for me; indeed, you were concerned for me, but had no opportunity to show it. [11]Not that I am referring to being in need; for I have learned to be content with whatever I have. [12]I know what it is to have little, and I know what it is to have plenty. In any and all circumstances I have learned the secret of being well-fed and of going hungry, of having plenty and of being in need. [13]I can do all things through him who strengthens me. [14]In any case, it was kind of you to share my distress.

I'm Fine

You have at last revived your concern for me. At last? It sounds like Paul is throwing a jab—how long must I waste away in prison before you show a little concern? But a better interpretation is that Paul is praising the Philippians. After all this time, for them to show concern for him, the Philippian congregation demonstrates the compassion that Paul has been talking about in this letter. As Paul lifted up Timothy and then Epaphroditus and finally himself as examples of faithfulness, now Paul points to the Philippians themselves as examples of humility and compassion. Their care for

Paul has been demonstrated in concrete fashion. They provided financial support for his ministry (Phil 4:15–18). They also sent Epaphroditus to minister to the apostle (Phil 4:18–19). For Paul to lift up these actions is not simply to address administrative matters or even to close the epistle with a thank-you note, but rather to point to the love of Christ alive in the Philippian congregation.

It is not too much to say that when Paul looks at this church, he sees Christ reflected in their shared life. In their concern for Paul, they are an example of having the mind of Christ. This is evident when he says, "I have learned the secret of being well-fed and of going hungry, of having plenty and of being in need." The secret is actually no secret to the Philippian church. It is the power to do all things through the strength of Christ (Phil 4:14). Again, this is not an abstract strength but an embodied strength. Paul is strengthened, because the Philippians have shown their concern for Paul.

The strength of Christ manifests itself in a spirit of contentment. Paul is content, because he has learned a faithful way to engage whatever the circumstances of his life may be. The circumstances do not determine his faith; his faith determines how he navigates the circumstances. So, whether well-fed or hungry, he knows that the God of peace guards his heart, and he is content.

This description of life echoes the wedding vow: I promise to be loving and faithful in plenty and in want, in joy and in sorrow, in sickness and in health. I love the honesty of that vow. The truth is, most of the time I have had the privilege to officiate a service where couples speak these vows, they do not seem to be compelled by the honesty of these words. They are so lost in themselves, I sometimes wonder if they even know I am standing right in front of them. But from my vantage point, I can see the friends and family who gather to share in the joyful occasion. Many who are witnesses to the marriage already made the same vows years earlier, maybe even decades earlier. It is in their eyes that I see a recognition of the honesty of the vow. They know that every human relationship faces good times and times of heartbreak. Every relationship knows joy and sorrow. At their best, every couple is promising and hoping and trusting that it is not the circumstances that shape their love for one another but, rather, their love for one another that helps them navigate the circumstances life will bring.

In a similar fashion, Paul is grateful for the love he knows from the congregation in Philippi. Their love that comes to him in his time of distress, rests on him as the love of Christ, is a love that strengthens him. It is because of their love that he can be content with little or plenty, with hunger or being well-fed.

Just over thirty years ago, my mother suffered a stroke. She was in her mid-fifties, had recently been ordained as a pastor, and was just beginning to build the life she anticipated after raising four children. The consequences of her stroke meant she couldn't work anymore. It also meant this articulate woman was robbed of almost all her vocabulary. If she wants a banana, she might end up asking for a toothbrush, or she might just say, "I need that thing." The condition is called aphasia and has led to some challenging conversations over the years, trying to interpret the message in the midst of the muddle. She clearly knows who I am, but she hasn't called me by name in over three decades. She just says, "Hey, love." This is also how she greets my wife, my sister, and Dorothy, the LPN who takes care of the rest of us by taking care of her.

One word my mother has never lost is "fine." Every time I ask her how she is doing, she is pretty quick to respond, "Oh, love, I'm fine." To be locked up inside yourself like that for decades would make a lot of folks bitter. To have language stripped away so that you can't hold the conversation a toddler could manage would frustrate even the most patient person. To have your mobility diminished and the friends of a lifetime slip past you at a pace you can no longer maintain would crush the spirit and maybe crucify any faith you had left. But I watch her with amazement as she greets more days than not with a sense of contentment. "I'm fine," she says.

When the apostle says "I have learned the secret," I believe him, because I have seen that secret strength in my own mother. She trusts that the God of peace is near and will stand guard, so that no ultimate harm will come.

Contentment and joy are not quite the same thing. But contentment is the music to which joy dances. Both contentment and joy come from a confidence that the love that makes sense of the world calls you by name.

Philippians 4:15–18

15You Philippians indeed know that in the early days of the gospel, when I left Macedonia, no church shared with me in the matter of giving and receiving, except you alone. 16For even when I was in Thessalonica, you sent me help for my needs more than once. 17Not that I seek the gift, but I seek the profit that accumulates to your account. 18I have been paid in full and have more than enough; I am fully satisfied, now that I have received from Epaphroditus the gifts you sent, a fragrant offering, a sacrifice acceptable and pleasing to God.

Gifts Matter

Paul received gifts from the Philippians. The gifts were brought to him by Epaphroditus. The financial gifts are important, for they not only help Paul survive and continue his ministry, but they are a concrete expression of love for the apostle. Epaphroditus himself was a gift as well. When life seems to attack you and you feel alone, nothing helps as much as a friend walking through the door. Epaphroditus comes to Paul, and in so doing, he carries the love of the entire church family. Paul is speaking in financial terms: "You shared with me in the matter of giving and receiving . . . sent me help for my needs more than once. Not that I seek the gift, but I seek the profit that accumulates to your account" (Phil 4:15–17). He talks like he is looking at his checkbook, but he is speaking from his heart. The Philippians have cared for Paul because they belong to one another. Paul doesn't call them family. He doesn't use that word, but he clearly understands their relationship as family, church family.

Brenda was a member of a small church family. Even though it was her practice to never miss worship on Sundays, when she became ill, she just didn't have it in her. The chemo was at the height of its destruction. She was tired, but it wasn't really the fatigue that kept her away. Her hair had fallen out. Everywhere she went, she wore a bandana. She wasn't vain, but she felt that every time she left the house she was announcing to the world that she was sick. She didn't want to go to church like that. It's not an uncommon reaction. Sometimes we find it harder to go to church when life has fallen apart. We assume that others are somehow more put together than we are, and that those around us are a collection of the smooth and shiny. But that's never the truth. The whole truth is that sometimes the body breaks. Sometimes the heart breaks. Sometimes our lives include that which we want hidden from view.

Brenda had some friends at church, rather obnoxious friends, who refused to take no for an answer. "You are coming to church. That's where you belong," they told her. She gave in. When Sunday arrived, she put her bandana on her fuzzy head and drove to church. When she arrived, there were fifteen or twenty women, all wearing bandanas. Two of them had shaved their heads. Church was not just where she went that morning; church was where she belonged. The journey with cancer was a journey that Brenda had to walk; no one could do that for her. But these women made sure she didn't walk it alone. It was a gift.

I am writing this in the middle of what the world knows as the coronavirus pandemic. For the past year and for an uncertain future, the church I serve has not had worship together in person. Each week, I walk into an empty sanctuary and preach to a little green light on a video camera. I know there are folks I love on the other side of that little green light. But the circumstance of shutdown has taught us in a very powerful way the basic need for human relationship. Even as fear of being in physical proximity poses a threat to health, the practice of being segregated from one another has heightened the awareness of our need for one another. The first story in the Good Book is the story of creation. And when God creates, everything is good, and good, and very good. The first thing that is declared not good is to be alone. We are learning that truth in new ways in the midst of this pandemic. The hunger for human contact is no doubt one that Paul shared. I imagine to have Epaphroditus walk through the door was as moving to Paul as it will be for the rest of us when we are able, at last, to open the doors of our sanctuary and welcome the church family to what will feel like a long overdue family reunion.

As we have said before, Jesus shows up in our relationships. Paul, who spent his ministry urging, encouraging, teaching, and at times almost demanding that people of faith care for our relationships, now finds himself on the receiving end of such love. It bolsters his confidence that the powers of the world may have put him in Caesar's prison, but he belongs to the love of God revealed in Christ, and that love is embodied in some saints that we can know only as the Philippians. For Paul, it was the evidence that God was doing a good thing in this world.

Philippians 4:19-23

[19]And my God will fully satisfy every need of yours according to his riches in glory in Christ Jesus. [20]To our God and Father be glory forever and ever. Amen.

[21]Greet every saint in Christ Jesus. The friends who are with me greet you. [22]All the saints greet you, especially those of the emperor's household.

[23]The grace of the Lord Jesus Christ be with your spirit.

Glory

As Paul concludes the letter, he turns to glory. It's an echo of some important paragraphs found earlier in the letter. In chapter 3, Paul promises that Christ will transform us into the body of his glory (Phil 3:21). We will be like him, and when we are, every need will be satisfied. That which is broken will be mended, that which is bruised will be comforted, that which is sinful will be turned around and made right. If I understand the text, the creation being made whole in glory is where Paul started, as he proclaimed his confidence that "the one who began a good work among you will bring it to completion by the day of Jesus Christ" (Phil 1:6). Until that day, we press on to obtain the resurrection, to make it our own, because Christ has made us his own (Phil 3:12).

This promised glory is not something for which we simply wait; it is something toward which we live. Most importantly, it is this promised future of God that has the power to shape our lives now. That means every day is shaped by hope.

Barbara Kingsolver's novel *Animal Dreams,* set in the 1980s, tells of two sisters, Codi and Hallie. Hallie traveles to Nicaragua to live there during a time when Nicaragua is embroiled in civil war. From her Central American experience, Hallie writes letters home to her sister, Codi. In one letter, Hallie writes,

> You're thinking of revolution as a great all-or-nothing. I think of it as one more morning in a muggy cotton field, checking the undersides of leaves to see what's been there, figuring out what to do that won't clear a path for worse problems next week. Right now that's what I do. You ask why I'm not afraid of loving and losing, and that's my answer . . . . The daily work—that goes on, it adds up . . . . Good things don't get lost.
>
> Codi, here's what I've decided: the very least you can do in your life is to figure out what you hope for. And the most you can do is live inside that hope. Not admire it from a distance but live right in it, under its roof. What I want is so simple I almost can't say it: elementary kindness. Enough to eat, enough to go around. The possibility that kids might one day grow up to be neither the destroyers nor the destroyed. That's about it. Right now I'm living in that hope, running down its hallway and touching the walls on both sides.
>
> I can't tell you how good it feels.[5]

5. Kingsolver, *Animal Dreams,* 299.

Hallie has learned what life is like when hope is discovered, even in the midst of a war-torn country. For Paul, the promised day defines every moment, every circumstance, every relationship. The day of Jesus Christ is our hope. Being in Christ, we see the world not only as it is but also as the power of Christ's redemptive love will make it. So each day brings a new moment to participate in the good. And the good things don't get lost. They add up. It's not a mechanical system but a mystical calculus in which the mercy of God gathers up the work of the faithful, and, in time, at the end of time, there is only good.

This hope also means we are not defined by that which is broken or injured. We are not defined by our failings and the wrongs we have committed. All of our failings and injuries are real and bring consequences that we must face. But we are defined by a holy love that calls us by name and will never let us go. That holy love, revealed in the humiliation and exaltation of Christ, will lead us and all to the promised day of God. This is why Paul sings a song of joy and why all things eventually lead to glory.

I traveled to the small town of Natchitoches, Louisiana. It is where the movie *Steel Magnolias* was filmed, and it is also where my brother lives. In the introduction, I mentioned my special needs brother, Gene. He lives in a group home and loves it. The care providers ensure his every need is met. He calls them his staff. The other residents are his family. Gene knows my name but prefers to call me brother or bwudah, as he pronounces it. As long as I can remember, Gene has had a dream. His dream is to drive a car. He wants to get behind the wheel of his car, preferably a red car. Sometimes he wants it to be a van, so he can crowd his buddies from the group home in with him, and they can take a road trip. When I had a dream like that, in my early teens, it was little more than the desire to simply hit the road. I was yearning for some freedom. But that's not the hunger behind my brother's dream. It's quite the opposite, in fact. He has a destination in mind—or several, I should say. His first trip will be to see our dad. He wants to surprise him, and I'm sure our dad would find nothing more surprising than to see Gene pull into the driveway. He then wants to visit our mom, who is in a nursing home. "She would love a visit from me," he says. Then he will travel to see his niece and nephew. I ask, "Gene, don't you want to come see me?" "You got your own car, Bwudah; you can come see me." So far, that's the only part of his dream that has come true. But whenever I visit him, he wants to talk about the visits he will make when he can finally drive. There has never been a moment in his life that has encouraged him to trust this dream.

On this particular visit, I took him out to dinner. We were eating at a hamburger joint called Shoney's Big Boy because Gene thinks that is fine dining. We both ordered the cholesterol plate. We talked about baseball and the Special Olympics. He had a medal he wanted to show me. We talked about his job washing windows and clearing tables at Burger King. He used to mow lawns, but he said it gets pretty hot in Louisiana. Eventually the conversation turned to what the conversation always turns to. "When I go see Daddy, don't you tell him; I want it to be a surprise." "I promise, brother, I won't say anything." "When I stop and get gas, I'm going to get a Coke, too," he said. We have rehearsed this conversation like it is liturgy from the prayer book. We talked about it when I turned sixteen and got my license. We talked about it when our little brother got his license. We talked about it when my kids got their licenses. But we never talked about it like we did that night at Shoney's. In a moment for which I was unprepared, he put his hamburger down and looked at me with level gaze and asked, "Bwudah, do you think I'll ever drive that car?"

He won't. He can't. He was dealt lesser cards. Some dreams are just that, dreams, and there is no amount of wanting them, no amount of believing in them, no amount of faith that will make them come true. So I told him the truth.

"Yes, Gene. The day will come when you will drive that car."

I know, he will never drive a car. He will certainly never drive my car. But that is not really what he was asking. In the end, it's not really about driving. It's more than that. He was asking the same question that people ask every day, particularly on their worst days. Will there ever come a day when all that has gone wrong will be made right? Will there ever come a day when God will at last keep every promise God has made? Will we ever find our way so that all do justice and love kindness and walk humbly with God? Will the prodigals find their way home and will the elder brothers learn to dance? Will the poor find their place at the feasting table? Will the failings and hurts and deep shames in all of our lives ever be washed away and forgotten? Will the good that God has begun in us and in the world ever come to completion? That's what he was asking. Like the old attorney Clarence Darrow, my brother was pleading for the future. And to that questioned plea, the answer is yes. The good work that God has begun will be brought to completion. That yes is the reason Paul sings of joy, even from

Caesar's prison cell. It is the reason we, too, in time, can know joy, even on our worst days. That is the hope Christ has given us. When you are able, live inside that hope right under its roof. Run down its hallway, touching it on both sides. When you do, sing glory.

A Final Word

THE WORD SPREAD THAT there was a letter from Paul. Someone asked, "When we gather for worship, who will read it to us?" "Maybe Epaphroditus. Maybe he has some additional instructions for us. Thank God he survived. It will be so good to see him again." "No, I think either Euodia or Syntyche will read it. They are our leaders." It was no small thing for women to be leaders anywhere in those days, but it was pretty common in the church. They were eager to hear what Paul had written. At last, a word from their leader and partner in the gospel. It was a big day. It was a day they had prayed for and waited for. And now, they all gathered together to hear this letter read for the first time.

So, how did that go?

There is no record of how the church responded to Paul's letter. If they wrote him back, that letter is lost. We have no news reports or even church newsletters opining on insights claimed from this correspondence. But we do know this: they kept this letter. And they shared it. Doing so is the reason we have the letter to the Philippians. New Testament scholar Eugene Boring has noted, "In what became mainstream Christianity, for the first one hundred years the letter form dominated Christian writing . . . .This early dominance of the letter form is a striking, unanticipated fact. In no other religious community have letters become sacred scripture or played such a formative role."[1]

As was noted in the introduction, the world that the first readers of this letter inhabited is dramatically different from the world in which we live. What has not changed is the struggle to be human in this world. For both them and us, the dance with grace remains an awkward one. To live lovingly with one another is no easier today than it was in Paul's day.

1. Boring, *Introduction to New Testament*, 196.

Caesar no longer holds any threat, but oppression remains. Injustice is constant. The climate threatens. Our children are anxious, and everyone knows someone with cancer. There is more meanness than there should be, and fear lurks behind everyday conversations. All that is to say, even though so much is different between our world and the old world of our Philippian ancestors, we are fortunate they were wise enough to pass this letter down to us. For in these ancient words, there is still truth for a fearful and self-absorbed generation.

They read the letter for the first time and had to be shocked—or, maybe because they knew him, they weren't too surprised. Paul rejoices. Even on his worst days, he holds fast to a conviction that the holy love that makes sense of life in this world has called him by name, and that is enough. Let us not forget this: it is fair to assume that the reason Paul writes so much about joy is because the Philippians themselves were lacking in joy. They were weighed down with the multiple crises in their lives. Their friend was in jail. Their leaders were in disagreement. And they trusted that Jesus was Lord, when seemingly everyone else on the planet was sure that a guy named Caesar was lord, and from the looks of who was calling the shots most days, Caesar was making a good case for himself. The Philippians would be forgiven if they moved through their lives a bit joyless. But it didn't have to stay that way. Paul would not have written so much about joy unless he believed that the Philippians could come to experience what he experienced. And if Paul had been wrong about that, and his words of inspiration had left them unchanged, and even after reading this letter they found themselves still captured by the shames and anxieties they had been carrying, then the Philippians would have had absolutely no reason to hang on to this letter. It would have found its way into the trash bin that collects Hallmark cards and pithy quotes from daily calendars. But we have this letter, so my bet is that when they read it (and reread it) something significant happened.

It still does.

Of course, it requires more than just reading.

My father talked about this only one time, that I can recall. He sat in the carport of our house, so that my sister and I would not see him crying. The day's mail arrived with an invoice for medical expenses. The amount of the invoice exceeded his annual salary. It was the last straw. The time was the fall of 1964, and he was pastor of a small congregation in Mississippi. The civil rights movement was everywhere, and what he called his modest support of that effort meant he was in conflict with some of the leaders in his church, and he could see the writing on the wall: the days were coming when he would no longer be their pastor. Just a few months before, he welcomed my sister, his one and only daughter, into the world. I was just old enough to render any room I was in a federally declared disaster area. My brother Gene was receiving inpatient care, as at eighteen months, he was still learning to swallow. My mother had crumbled under the weight of severe postpartum depression and was hospitalized. Taking care of three small children, his wife suffering greatly, and uncertainty about his vocational future was hard. It was, no doubt, one of my father's worst days. When the mail arrived with the unpayable invoice, it pushed him over the edge. He went to the carport to weep.

The details vary with any life, but everyone walks through the storm. Those last straw days come to everyone. When they do, most of us crumble. It's like the world unzips our chest, and all our strength and courage spill out of us and splatter all over the floor, and we are left empty. That's what happened to my dad that fall day in 1964.

But what he did next changed his life. He said he prayed. Not a pretty prayer book kind of prayer. Like Job, he yelled at God. He vented his fear and his pain. He let God know just how disappointing God had been. And then he made a decision. He would begin tithing. Crazy, right? He already gave money to support the church, but he decided to adopt the old practice of giving 10 percent of his income to the work of the church. He hoped that if he gave that much away, he would have control of his finances rather than his finances having control of him. It was just one pressure point on his heart in the fall of 1964, but it was a turning point.

My mother got better. My brother learned to swallow. Eventually the unpayable bill was paid. My dad did have to resign, but another congregation called him to serve them. Let me be clear, this is not one of those prosperity gospel fairytales that you find on religious broadcasts. This is not a claim that tithing is an investment program where God promises to make you heathy and wealthy, like there is some kind of heavenly index fund with hundredfold returns. My point is much more basic than that: faith is practiced. Faith is lived out in daily choices, and when life falls apart, those ordinary practices, like prayer, worship, and even tithing—among many others—can become a great source of strength. My dad never stopped tithing, and he taught me to do the same from the time I started making an allowance for clearing the dinner dishes from the table and making my bed in the mornings. It became a source of deep satisfaction for him and for me, too. Generosity is a source of joy.

Joy that we claim on our worst days will not just come to us; it will be the result of faithful practices in our lives. Joy is not just an experience; it is also a discipline.

The Marshmallow Test

During the 1960s, a Stanford University psychologist, Walter Mischel, conducted an experiment with children who were four years old. It was called the marshmallow test. A researcher placed a child in a room with an edible treat, like a marshmallow. The child was told that the researcher needed to step out of the room for a moment but would return. When the researcher returned, she would then give the child permission to eat the treat. But here's the trick: if the child just couldn't wait, he or she could ring a bell, the researcher would return immediately, and the child could enjoy the treat. But, if the child waited until the researcher returned on her own, the child could have the treat, and a second treat as well.

Unsurprisingly, Mischel discovered that some children could postpone gratification and earn a second treat, and others barely allowed the researcher to get out of the room before the bell was rung. Mischel followed up with the same children a decade or so later and discovered that those who demonstrated a degree of self-control with the marshmallow tended to be doing better in life as teenagers.

But something else was discovered as well. Those who demonstrated the discipline to wait did not just sit in their chairs and watch the door until the researcher returned. "The strategies the strong-willed kids employed to resist temptation were remarkable. Some covered the marshmallow up with a napkin, while others sang songs. What was on display, Michel concluded, were the various strategies that humans of all ages use to delay gratification."[2]

Delaying gratification is a common experience and a skill that can enrich one's daily life. My mother taught me that I could watch TV, but only after I finished my spelling homework. Certain disciplines can be engaged to help postpone joy from the present into the future. But can the reverse occur? Can similar practices be employed not to push a current joy into

2. Dunkelman, *Vanishing Neighbor*, 214.

the future, but to bring a future joy into the present, when there is not a marshmallow to be found for miles around?

Joy is sometimes an experience. Joy sometimes captures us, even overwhelms us, and it is unavoidable. This is the only way I know to describe my response to the birth of my children or even the first time I was called to serve a congregation. Those were joyful days. But joy that is simply an experience is hard to sustain during the worst days. On the harder days, joy must be pursued. It is chosen. Joy that will sustain us during difficult times must be the result of practices that nourish the spirit and strengthen the soul.

We Are Stronger Than We Thought

This little book began as a collection of videos Village Church produced for Bible study groups. Small groups would meet together, watch the videos, and discuss things that matter to them. It's an important part of our ministry every year. But then, circumstances pushed me deeper into this conversation with Paul. The worst days seemed to be stacking up. I have written this during the year of the pandemic. The challenges of this year have been unparalleled in many ways. The realities of COVID-19 have created isolation, job loss, illness, and death. In one year of COVID, almost as many Americans have died as did during four years of the Civil War. Most people in the world know someone who has died from this virus. Most died surrounded not by loved ones but by critical care nurses. The fortunate had the strength to make one last FaceTime call to say goodbye. It has also been a year when the normal rituals to address grief have been compromised. The community couldn't gather for services to give thanks for the life of loved ones and claim again the promise of the resurrection. Zoom services have been a gift when there was no other alternative, but we were all keenly aware of our hunger for the alternative.

When the air we breathe poses a threat, it erodes our normal practices of friendship. That has been challenging enough. And then, our attention and grief turned toward those who couldn't breathe at all. We watched George Floyd die before us. His name joined a long list of those who have died needlessly. A season of protest and lament erupted all across the nation. Many, including myself, had assumed we as a nation had at least agreed on the trajectory regarding race in America; but that was naïve. Groups committed to the myth of white supremacy reemerged with surprising strength.

This year also included an election cycle that revealed not simply the polarization that is commonplace in contemporary America, but, even more concerning, it became evident that there is no shared civic narrative in the country. With many depending on siloed news reports that exist to reinforce ideological armies, we find it more than challenging to agree not only on the significance of events but even on what the facts of a given circumstance might be.

For these and other reasons, 2020 has been a brutal year, a year we are eager to leave in the rearview mirror. But not so fast. We cannot afford to leave this year behind without learning the lessons that such difficulties might teach us.

In the midst of the heartbreak, the fracture, the anger, and the grief that was 2020, there were signs of grace—ordinary folks who lived as messengers of grace. Everywhere we looked, there were people, some of whom we may not have noticed before, but during this season of testing they shone like bright lights of courage and strength.

In the early days of quarantine, when I was still wiping down the milk and the can of black beans when I got home from the grocery store, I spoke to Dorothy, who was the cashier. Only her eyes were visible over her mask, but they betrayed her anxiety. "Thank you for being here," I said. "Of course, I know you need to eat," she said. She is an angel.

The doctors and nurses who have lived in a state of exhaustion fighting against increasing odds to keep themselves safe while they heal the sick, they, too, are angels. But so are the people in the cafeteria who are preparing meals for the sick and the quiet employees in the environmental services department who kept the hospital rooms clean and sterile. But not just them: all the scientists who raced the clock to create a vaccine and the thousands of volunteers who rolled up their sleeves to participate in vaccine trials, they are ordinary people who demonstrated extraordinary courage.

What I noticed is that the more I paid attention to the courage displayed in my neighbors, the stronger I felt myself. It seemed as if the fingerprints of God were all around us, nourishing a deep humanness in the face of hardship. We learned we were stronger than we thought. There are lessons about the work of God in the world that we learn in the valley of the shadow. These lessons are harder to know when all things are bright and beautiful. And one of those lessons is that joy is possible, even on our worst days. But it takes practice. It comes from, among other things, remembering that God is at work in you, doing a good work that will be brought to completion. And like a four-year-old child who sings a song to get through the long winter of the researcher's departure, faith has given us practices that carry us through the difficult seasons. If we are fortunate, we also have friends like Epaphroditus, who come to us in the hard times. There are also memories of how God has been our help in ages past, so will be our hope for years to come.[3] There are simple practices, like writing a letter, to recount to the faithful that the gospel is alive, even in these days. Your practices may vary, but to get through the difficult times with a spirit of joy requires the discipline of a practiced faith.

By the time you read this, I hope the challenges of 2020 are a distant memory. But whenever you read this, there will be trouble enough in the world. Each generation inherits challenges handed down from those who have gone before, problems left unaddressed. And each generation creates problems anew, some of which are passed on to the next generation. Individually, every life faces the realities of broken dreams and broken hearts, of fragile bodies and personal failings. All of us have that list of griefs that are hard to shake, shames that are hard to lay down, and disappointments that are difficult to forget. In short, you will have your worst days. On those days, it will be helpful to hold fast to what this old preacher from prison can teach us.

In a somewhat intentional fashion, I have written this reflection on Philippians as an effort to train my own heart to be more intentional about harvesting the fruit of joy. In truth, it has made me a more joyful person. From Paul's example, I have learned several lessons. Even in prison, he claims that he belongs to Christ, and in every circumstance, he can participate in the ministry of the gospel. Paul is attentive to his friendships and counts them as gifts, and from them draws strength. Paul is humble and looks for the good in others, for it is there that he most clearly sees the presence of Christ in the world. But mostly, Paul trusts that the good work that God has begun in him, in the Philippian congregation and in the world, will someday, some grand and glorious day, be brought to completion (Phil 1:6). He spends every day living toward that promised day. At the end of the day, and at the end of our days, that is the reason for joy.

Now that you have read Paul's letter, do what his first readers did: hold on to it, and also pass it on.

3. Watts, "O God, Our Help."

Bibliography

Alexander, Michelle. *The New Jim Crow: Mass Incarceration in the Age of Colorblindness.* Rev. ed. New York: New, 2012.

Backman, Fredrik. *Us against You.* New York: Washington Square, 2018.

Barth, Karl. *The Epistle to the Philippians.* Richmond, VA: John Knox, 1962.

Beker, J. Christiaan. *Paul the Apostle: The Triumph of God in Life and Thought.* Philadelphia: Fortress, 1980.

Bellah, Robert N. *Habits of the Heart: Individualism and Commitment in American Life.* Berkeley, CA: University of California Press, 1985.

Berry, Wendell. *Jayber Crow.* Berkeley, CA: Counterpoint, 2000.

Boring, M. Eugene. *An Introduction to the New Testament: History, Literature, Theology.* Louisville: Westminster John Knox, 2012.

Botton, Alain de. "Why You Will Marry the Wrong Person." *New York Times,* May 29, 2016. https://www.nytimes.com/2016/05/29/opinion/sunday/why-you-will-marry-the-wrong-person.html.

Bowler, Kate. *Everything Happens for a Reason: And Other Lies I've Loved.* New York: Random House, 2018.

Brooks, David. *The Road to Character.* New York: Random House, 2015.

———. *The Second Mountain: The Quest for a Moral Life.* New York: Random House, 2019.

Broyles, William, Jr. *Cast Away.* Directed by Robert Zemeckis. Los Angeles: Twentieth-Century Fox, 2000.

Buechner, Frederick. *The Longing for Home: Recollections and Reflections.* New York: HarperCollins, 1996.

Burns, Jennifer. *Goddess of the Market: Ayn Rand and the American Right.* New York: Oxford University Press, 2009.

Collins, Jim. *Good to Great: Why Some Companies Make the Leap . . . and Others Don't.* New York: Collins, 2001.

Craddock, Fred B. *Philippians.* Interpretation: A Bible Commentary for Teaching and Preaching. Atlanta: John Knox Press, 1985.

Dickens, Charles. *A Tale of Two Cities.* Reprint, London, WI: Octopus Books Limited, 1985.

Dunkelman, Marc J. *The Vanishing Neighbor: The Transformation of American Community.* New York: W.W. Norton & Company, 2014.

Eberhardt, Jennifer L. *Biased: Uncovering the Hidden Prejudice That Shapes What We See, Think, and Do.* New York: Viking, 2019.

Bibliography

Friend, Tad. "Silicon Valley's Quest to Live Forever: Can Billions of Dollars' Worth of High-Tech Research Succeed in Making Death Optional?" *New Yorker Magazine,* Mar 27, 2017. https://www.newyorker.com/magazine/2017/04/03/silicon-valleys-quest-to-live-forever.

Graetz, Michael J., and Linda Greenhouse. *The Burger Court and the Rise of the Judicial Right.* New York: Simon & Schuster, 2016.

Grisham, John. *Innocent Man: Murder and Injustice in a Small Town.* New York: Doubleday, 2006.

Hooker, Morna D. "The Letter to the Philippians: Introduction, Commentary, and Reflections." In Vol. 11 of *The New Interpreter's Bible,* edited by Leander E. Keck et al., 467–549. Nashville: Abingdon, 2000.

Howell, Elizabeth. "How Many Stars Are in the Universe?" https://www.space.com/26078-how-many-stars-are-there.html.

Hunter, James Davison. *To Change the World: The Irony, Tragedy, and Possibility of Christianity in the Late Modern World.* New York: Oxford University Press, 2010.

Irving, John. *A Prayer for Owen Meany.* New York: William Morrow, 2012.

Kidd, Sue Monk. *The Secret Life of Bees.* New York: Penguin, 2002.

King, Martin Luther, Jr. "I See the Promised Land." In *A Testament of Hope: The Essential Writings of Martin Luther King Jr.,* edited by James Melvin Washington, 279–86. San Francisco: Harper & Row, 1986.

Kingsolver, Barbara. *Animal Dreams.* New York: HarperPerennial, 1991.

Küng, Hans. *On Being a Christian.* Translated by Edward Quinn. New York: Image, 1984.

Labberton, Mark. *Called: The Crisis and Promise of Following Jesus Today.* Downers Grove, Il: InterVarsity, 2014.

Lama, Dalai, et al. *The Book of Joy: Lasting Happiness in a Changing World.* New York: Avery, 2016.

Larson, Edward J., and Jack Marshall, eds. *The Essential Words and Writings of Clarence Darrow.* New York: Modern Library, 2007.

Long, Thomas G. *What Shall We Say?: Evil, Suffering, and the Crisis of Faith.* Grand Rapids: Eerdmans, 2011.

Lowry, James S. *Low-Back, Ladder-Back, Cane-Bottom Chair.* Winona, MN: Saint Mary's,1999.

Lowry, Robert. "How Can I Keep from Singing." https://hymnary.org/text/my_life_flows_on_in_endless_song.

Marche, Stephen. "Is Facebook Making Us Lonely?" *Atlantic* (May 2012). https://www.theatlantic.com/magazine/archive/2012/05/is-facebook-making-us-lonely/308930/.

McClure, Bruce. "How Far Is a Light Year?" https://earthsky.org/astronomy-essentials/how-far-is-a-light-year.

Meacham, Jon. *His Truth Is Marching On: John Lewis and the Power of Hope.* New York: Random House, 2020.

Mecchi, Irene, et al. *The Lion King.* Directed by Roger Allers and Ron Minkoff. Burbank, CA: Walt Disney Pictures, 1994.

Migliore, Daniel L. *Philippians and Philemon.* Louisville: Westminster John Knox, 2014.

Miles, C. Austin. "In the Garden." https://hymnary.org/text/i_come_to_the_garden_alone.

Millard, Candice. *The River of Doubt: Theodore Roosevelt's Darkest Journey.* New York: Doubleday, 2005.

McCullough, David. *John Adams.* New York: Simon and Schuster, 2001.

Bibliography

North, John. "Got Class." In Vol. 3 of *Open to the Sky: An Anthology*, edited by Arlin Buyert, 19. Kansas City: Covington Group, 2018.

O'Connor, Flannery. *The Complete Stories*. New York: Farrar, Straus and Giroux, 1971.

Ottati, Douglas F. *Reforming Protestantism: Christian Commitment in Today's World.* Louisville: Westminster John Knox, 1995.

Putnam, Robert D. *Bowling Alone: The Collapse and Revival of American Community.* New York: Simon & Schuster, 2000.

Rand, Ayn. "Why Selfishness?" In *The Ayn Rand Reader,* edited by Gary Hull and Leonard Peikoff, 79–83. New York: Plumb, 1999.

Reilly, Rick. "Worth the Wait." *Sports Illustrated,* Oct. 20, 2003. https://vault.si.com/vault/2003/10/20/worth-the-wait.

Sampley, J. Paul. "Reasoning from the Horizons of Paul's Thought World: A Comparison of Galatians and Philippians." In *Theology and Ethics in Paul and His Interpreters,* edited by Eugene H. Lovering Jr. et al., 114–31. Nashville: Abingdon, 1996.

Sandel, Michael J. *Justice: What's the Right Thing to Do?* New York: Farrar, Straus and Giroux, 2009.

Smith, James K. A. *On the Road with Saint Augustine: A Real-World Spirituality for Restless Hearts.* Grand Rapids: Brazor, 2019.

Spufford, Francis. *Unapologetic: Why, Despite Everything, Christianity Can Still Make Surprising Emotional Sense.* New York: HarperOne, 2012.

Stendahl, Krister. *Paul among Jews and Gentiles, and Other Essays.* Philadelphia: Fortress, 1976.

Stevenson, Bryan. *Just Mercy.* New York: Spiegel & Grau, 2014.

Tamez, Elsa. *Philippians, Colossians, Philemon.* Edited by Barbara E. Reid et al. Wisdom Comentary 51. Collegeville, MN: Liturgical, 2017.

Taylor, Barbara Brown. *Leaving Church: A Memoir of Faith.* New York: Harper Collins, 2006.

Thurston, Bonnie B., and Judith M. Ryan. *Philippians and Philemon.* Edited by Daniel J. Harrington. Sacra Pagina 10. Collegeville, MN: Liturgical, 2005.

Tolstoy, Leo. *Anna Karenina.* Translated by Richard Pevear and Larissa Volokhonsky. New York: Penguin Classics, 2000.

Tyson, Neil DeGrasse. *Astrophysics for People in a Hurry.* New York: W. W. Norton & Co., 2017.

Utech, Jack. "Letter from the Philippines." In *The Church Monthly,* newsletter of Riverside Church, New York, Mar. 1945.

Viorst, Judith, *Alexander and the Terrible, Horrible, No Good, Very Bad Day.* New York: Antheneum Books for Young Readers, 1972.

Watts, Isaac. "O God, Our Help in Ages Past." https://hymnary.org/text/our_god_our_help_in_ages_past_watts.

Weir, Ben, et al. *Hostage Bound, Hostage Free.* Philadelphia: Westminster, 1987.

Wesley, Charles. "Love Divine, All Loves Excelling." https://hymnary.org/text/love_divine_all_love_excelling_joy_of_he.

Whyte, David. *Consolations: The Solace, Nourishment and Underlying Meaning of Everyday Words.* Langley, WA: Many Rivers, 2015.

Made in the USA
Monee, IL
21 February 2024

53845585R00075